COMMONS

Poems 2017-2019

for Ken Irby - Keith Wilson
Rosalie Sorrels - Bobbie Louise Hawkins
Stephen Rodefer - Bill Pearlman
Latif Harris - Jim Fish
in memory

~ ♡ ~

Earth in Oligarchal Grip - 2017
Thunder - 2018
Early Riser - 2019

LARRY GOODELL

© 2020 Larry Goodell
All Rights Reserved

by the poet
A New Land & Other Writings (prose), 205 pp, duende press 2019.
Hot Art & Other Plays, 222 pp, duende press 2019.
Nothing to Laugh About, poems 2015-2016, 177 pp, Beatlick Press 2018.
Pieces of Heart, poems 2014, 140 pp; *Digital Remains* poems 2013, 157 pp;
Broken Garden & The Unsaid Sings, poems 2011-2012, 196 pp, (3 books)
    Beatlick Press 2015.
Here On Earth, 59 Sonnets, 96 pp, La Alameda Press, New Mexico 1996.
Out of Secrecy, poems by Larry Goodell, 22 pp, Yoo-Hoo Press 1992.
Firecracker Soup, poems 1980-1987, 103 pp, Cinco Puntos Press 1990.
The Mad New Mexican (Songs 1981-86) Ubik Sound 1986.
Dawn Ladder, a long poem, San Marcos Press Chapbook 1981?
Sunlove Gypsy, a long poem, duende press 1967.
Cycles, author's first book, edited and with a foreword by William
    Harris, duende press 1966.
Online Publications - larrygoodell.wordpress.com, larry goodell.com,
    duende.bandcamp.com/

credits
Cover photograph by the poet, design by Lenore Goodell.
    Drawings by the poet.
"Qué Pasa Picasso" published in *Survival,* John Roche Editor, Beatlick
    Press 2018.
"Here We Are," "Pills for Poetica," "Democracy" published in *Fixed
    and Free,* Poetry Anthology 2018, 10th Anniversary Collection.
"Ever Present," "Vowels and Vows," " Scimitar," "No Muse" published
    in *Unlikely Stories,* Mark V.
Photo on last page is by Lenore Goodell.

note
There are several sonnets in this collection which I define only as
    poems having 14 lines.

duende press
placitas, new mexico, usa 2020

COMMONS
EARTH IN OLIGARCHAL GRIP - 2017

Looking For Common Sense.... 1	3 - Too Late................... 35
Moral Ground............... 2	4 - Meeting Jim Fish........... 35
The Last Violator 2	5 - Dark Father 36
This Will Only Take A Minute . 3	6 - Among All Colors 36
To Speak About Love......... 4	7 - Death Thinking............. 37
Swell Fire of Light 5	8 - Not Camping............... 37
Jot........................ 6	9 - Harvest.................... 38
Superb Be 7	10 - A Time To Open My Heart... 39
The Older You Get........... 9	11 - Go On 39
Artichokes of Pluperfect Gods 10	12 - Meditations Under Venus.... 40
Looking for Common Sense ... 11	13 - Venus Warns 41
What Am I Going to Do...... 12	14 - What Who 42
Lack Of 13	15 - Going In, Getting Out...... 43
Poet Power 14	16 - No Muse 43
Be Be 15	17 - Brotherly.................. 44
Miss Malfunction 16	Phoenix - From the Ashes....... 45
Who I Am Not 17	Fairy Tale: Beast of Zozar 46
Baron Fracas Von Fuckus 17	Impetus On................... 47
Earth in Oligarchal Grip 18	Scimitar...................... 47
Mother of Ancient God 19	Cheap Shots 48
The Ghastly Remains......... 20	Bathroom Humor.............. 49
Keep the Poor from the Door . 20	Gift of Unknowing 50
"Citizens United" 21	Wrong Direction 50
Hubba Hubba............... 21	A Normal Day................. 51
Lie the Truth to Death....... 22	The Harmony of Tao 52
Stealth Bombers 22	Vowels and Vows 54
Wealthy Healthy Says 23	Waking Up Too Early 54
Educate 23	Felicitous Dharma 55
Arch Directive............... 23	The Fountain Of *No Muse*....... 56
Don't Do It 24	Qué Pasa Picasso? 58
Critique 25	Suddenly the Sky Falling Doors .. 60
Birth Of Song 26	Repair 60
For Kathy................... 28	Church of Reality 61
Unconscious Sonnet 28	Return Home 62
Dawn or Not................ 29	Myth Mother.................. 64
Through The Trees........... 30	What Tragedy?................ 65
Morning Star - 17 Poems 34	Exiles 65
1 - June 6th & On 34	Mitosis....................... 66
2 - Longing 34	Not Too Late.................. 67

An Offer 68	Noise Bank 82
Fragile Grace 68	Half Wish 83
Best Shared 69	Tums. 83
Ongoing 70	This Room 84
Machismo. 71	Getting Low 85
The Bruisers 71	Like Me. 85
Matriarchs: A Note 72	You And I. 86
For Ann 73	Closest One 90
Common As the Rare 74	Mantra Of Care 91
October 24 75	Good Morning, *Prayer* – 92
Tense 76	Fizznew 93
We Sonnet 76	Bye Bye Net neutrality 94
Mountain Top 77	Masculine Spirit 95
Repetition 77	Belief. 96
Door To Door. 78	The Song In You 96
A Place of Skulls 79	Dawn Song. 97
They're Glad You're Poor 79	The Light Bounces Through. 97
Collusion 80	Morning. 98
End Times 80	Water Creek Swallowtails. 99
Transmission 81	Loving Someone 100

THUNDER - 2018

Water Chant 101	Ms. Nature. 114
Mono Color 102	Conversations 115
They Threw Me Out 103	In Love. 116
Here and Now 103	Hallelujah 116
Scattering Voice 104	Criminal Crapola 117
Gravitational Waves 106	Musing About It 118
Accident Pleasure 106	Primary 118
Handshake. 107	Deception 118
Be The Light Within 108	Brothers and Sisters 119
One to Another 108	Students. 119
It's Better to Love 109	Talk It Out 120
On The Physical 109	For Lenore. 121
Hormonal Blast 110	Immensity 121
The Bruisers. 108	Listening to Schoenberg 122
The Learning Curve of Death. 111	Diversity 122
What Was Our Face 111	The Dawning – 2018 123
Particles of Wisdom 112	Journal Page 124
Dark Interior 112	Mother Nature 125
Pop Music 112	He. 126
Flavor of Innocense. 113	Loner Freedom 126
Ah 114	Love in Quotes 127

What Is Love 127	No Nada 150
A Patchwork of Enigma 128	From Memory 151
Good Hands 128	Youthful Gain, ... 152
Gun Down 129	Leaving Roswell 152
Going Forward 130	Dumb Fuck 153
Deflation 130	Absent 153
Poetica Pills 131	Judge Brat Year of the Man 154
Nature's Miracle Pill 131	Brat's Notes 155
What Is the Screw 132	Anal Party 155
Democracy 132	Guiding Eyes 156
Heterosapien 133	Solo Dancer 156
Silence 134	On Laboring at Meditation 156
Did You Say Garden? 134	Rescue Next To You 157
One More Year 135	First One 157
DeKooning Buddhism 136	In Good Hands 158
Secretly I Love Openly 136	Rainbow Speaking 161
Known To Be Known 137	Wealth Sickness 161
The Mind Carries On Love . . 137	Love Unfolds 162
Pray(se) 138	Exactly the Same 162
Oh Aurora 140	Ever Present 163
In The Valley 141	Wishful Thinking 165
Get It Right With Him 142	Belled Out 166
US Is the Underbelly 143	They All Have Mothers 166
Unstuck 143	Bye Bye Dogma 166
Here We Are 144	Directions 167
Healing Time 145	As The Stars Tell 167
Nature Itself 146	Inflated Doodad 168
America's Problem 147	Open to Secret 170
2018 Etiquette 147	Queen Of Everything 171
Gentle Rain 148	Less Rotten New Year 172
Curiosity 149	

EARLY RISER - 2019

Mother of Vast Decree 174	We Know Nothing 181
Do Not Give Up Football 176	Reflection of the Universe 181
Walking On My Bones 176	Mystery Caller 182
Impossibly Blue 176	What To Do 183
Tufts 177	Uh Oh 183
Loss Is Gain 177	Moralitee 184
A New Leaf 178	I Couldn't Lie 186
Spica They Tell Me 179	My Derriere 187
That Humility 180	Fondling Music 187
Beast 180	What Turns Here & Now 188

Tired of Living? 189	Death of a Hummingbird 209
Underlying Love 190	Game 210
The Bounds of Love 190	Who It Is 211
Why Tell Him 191	It is Me I Write It Down 211
The Culture of Sweep 191	12 Step Breath 212
Hills of Tech 192	After Thoughts 213
Moon 192	Greed Über Alles 214
Blockage? 192	What Happened 214
Hurting Out 193	HONOR, The Winning Soul 214
Answers 193	Welcoming Signs 215
Recompense 194	Fake Manikin 216
Pulling Through 195	The Winning Soul 217
Want: A Human Being 196	Slobber Love 218
Lufu Lubo Liebe 197	The Center 218
Dumpette 198	Shouting At The Muse 219
Goal 199	How To 220
Early Riser 199	Honor 222
Teeter-Totter 200	Dreaming 223
Archival Laughter 200	Unheeded Advice 224
In The Air 201	It Is Free 225
Orion 202	Have We Been Here? 226
Loved, Loved 203	Republican Counsel 229
The Now of Good 204	He Did It 230
Fall/Winter Trends 206	A Note From Busy Barb 230
Worse Than Any Skunk 207	Candle 1 231
A Peach 207	Candle 2 231
Joseph E. Tweezers 208	Desert Song 232
Cacophony of Music 209	

My songs lie concealed
In the secrets
And surprises
That are yet to be revealed

/from "Twenty-Five" in *Firemiles*, 1975
          Jim Fish

COMMONS

∼♡∼

"No decisions should ever be made
without asking the question,
is this for the common good?"
Michael Moore

LARRY GOODELL

EARTH IN OLIGARCHAL GRIP
Poems - 2017

Looking for Common Sense

Celebrity and Billionaire worship
has become a spur in the side of
the thorn in the flesh.
The mind rots on it and humility
becomes a poison. With too many people
strangling the planet and sending mounds
of CO_2 up in the air
the petro-billionaires famously dine on lies
Earth struggles to breathe and maintain
any equilibrium.
What do brains have to do
with money and fame?
Rational thought process, common sense,
where are you?

Moral Ground

I can put up with anything except
the "falsified look" of truth –
the danger of deception overrules
and spreads through norm.
Normalize shit pies and call them apple.
Jawohl!
Reduce the level of discourse to scum
and call it boys will be boys.
Accepting lying never for me not that I'm
a guardian of truth but I have an aim –
always to be accurate to what is
and allow compassion to flow.

The Last Violator

The news is views of pews empty in
the Church of Truth as we gaze on
we wonder why truth vacated.
There is no one in the church.
The priest is deported.
The organ has been sold.
The pews are being lifted out
one by one.
There's no place to sit.
There's nobody.
They're all out under the big tent
for the Revival of Death.
Hypocrisy is their preacher
And Obscure, the choir.
The new pews are benches of Falsehood.
The offertory is to pay for Lies.
"This is the Way" is all you hear.
"This is the Way."
This is the way to death and destruction
I say as they come for me.
This is the way to destroy
the Human Spirit.   /28Jan2017

This Will Only Take A Minute

"There are ways to test the universe
to see if it's worthy of yourself.
Does it provide you with a home
and loved ones?
Food on the table and a shopping list?
A job, an aim to do good?
Or does it deny you everything and turn
your life upside down
give you agony and defeat
crossing the hairs of your head
and filling your head with emptiness?

"There are ways to test the universe
but then, does it even care?
Is care built into every atom?
Every proton, every star?
Tell me who knows and I'll tell you nobody knows.
So how is the universe on a scale from 1 to 10?
If you're rich and absurdly comfortable, a 10.
(But then you'd want so much more, maybe a 5.)
If you're miserable and can't provide for yourself
and at your wit's end, give it a 1.
Now, on a scale from 1 to 10 how would you
    rate this phone call?"

To Speak About Love

If I don't speak about love
my heart is in the wrong place
my body is tired
and depression hails from loneliness.
There is the object of affection
right around the corner
or in the same room
or in memory alive forever.

That glowing figure is there
in the neighborhood
or across the way
or here to stay
to draw me out
into the harboring feeling
of encompassing love,
always coming from me
whether returned or not.

Emanations are half the secret.
Free to have them,
let all go out
naturally.
That great source
sunlight of love
I cannot smother
or cover
 or deny the opening
  touch
   or deny the range of affection
    you give me
     whether here or not.
      Source burns
       and gives
        grace of itself
         *out to the warmly
         deserved.*

Swell Fire of Light – Blue Spruce Yoga

Swell fire of light that ascends the body in remaking the day, brother of breathing lifting the hands high above the head, the arms stretching out to catch that high spirit and relax as it journeys down, hands arms out from high, side arcs all the way down to the knees. Pillar of body now become less solid. As noise noises out, noise is non-existent. Instead there is air movement.

What rises through is the *grace* you can never figure out, the fullness of the emptiness that ties you to voices long before you and, freely given, freely comes and goes and gives when everything else takes away, the personal lift that connects to what sincerely matters to this day, to this time, the unaccountable sublime unknown known, what whispering presence or part of one's own body speaks from within, without outside, in an occasional connection to *all that matters*.

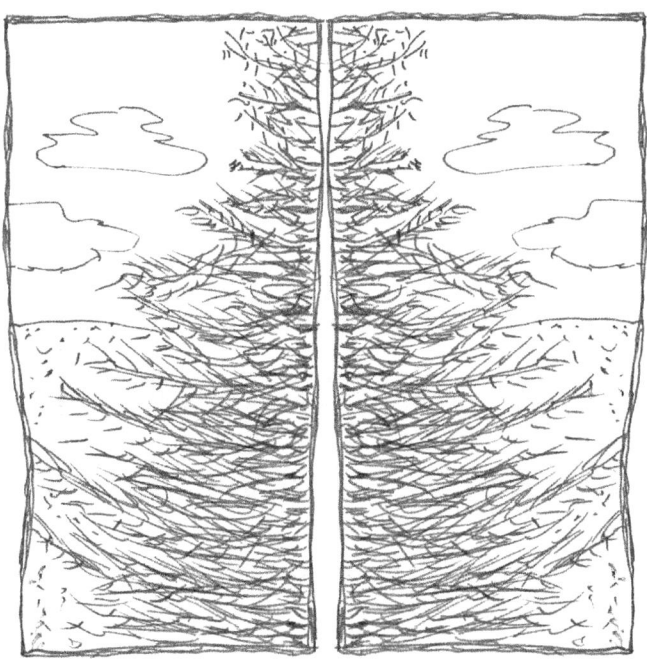

Jot

As a token of learning we left our heart in the palm of our ears
yes it was open to receive but no one came.
Time collapsed as Einstein and Stephen Hawkins met.
The mind began to discover patterns of its own
down in ancient mysteries that needed a touch of science
    to freshen up new discoveries.
Aha was met with aha was met with *aha*.
But the fighting evacuated everyone from the laboratories.
The streets rose up and became perpendicular to science.
At the point where they met, all progress stopped.
Only art was left that wasn't in museums or galleries.

Those quiet gnomes of creativity unbarred
    untied to anything but
the true faith, unheard of connections to the far
    inner galaxy never to be discovered
but bursting in vibrant unknown communication.
The true hand, expression of the true male-female mind
the journal in the very back of the cave brought out into the light
    by the mountain stream.

Superb Be

"It almost becomes like a sign of fear when I see anyone repressing being able to enjoy something like color."
- Jeffrey Gibson, artist, from an interview 2011.

(This poem came from seeing and hearing Jeffrey Gibson's exhibit at Site in Santa Fe and was displayed as part of the exhibit. My drawing is of the ceremonial atttire worn by Mr. Gibson.)

Shaman white blithering sainthood
   rapid fire egg hunting at Easter
Christmas turquoise tree ornaments
   and ancient roots severed from all trees
in fear of the future laughing hard
   from death's head in a colorful breeze
give me a rhyme to the past at last
   to the present pheasant that disappeared
when you shot at an elk that wasn't there any more
   what's slipping out from under you if not

the last ice age the beaded punching bags
   descending from the ceiling and swinging
swing low sweet chariot of the Muse
   she lost her forelocks her sister her reason
to be amused for you, she screams like Medusa
   "you poisoned my water" the water falls from the
Virgin of Guadalupe
   and waters Mother Earth, Tlaloc nods
Chalchiutlicue appears in the cenotes,
   acequia running runs off in farmland now
garden land, now overgrown weeds, tumbleweeds
   sunflowers give a mind to the past
covered with bells, tinkle bells and rattles covered with
   layers of covered tinkle-rattling bells as the god
approaches the white board and writes messages
   everybody can understand: "Jump Into the Void"
"Transform like a butterfly"
   the remarkable ethno-poetic towel dispenser
automatically washes your hands before it
   dries them as cars fly by themselves to their previous dawn
and the performance of ethno-strut does
   fancy footwork to trance rave beat beat
volcanic electronic power bump speakers and
   gong drums look out red radiating eyes
to the white men passing by the black ladies all colors
   up and down humanoids lost their future
splashing mish-mash of colors as lost hope
   powering wowing you better appreciate
flashing dancing before you labor intensive
   gift on gift as sound on foot
colors for the joy of it on rawhide
   hide nothing, present themselves in
drums and walls, pieces, elaborate spreading out
   garments or propped up
presentation of itself in tea time
   Indian time tune tomorrow today

served on a palette beads dropping delicately
   in every position the organized mind
shouts out patterns full hanging tassels
   tessellated beads of no time now
now of no time is now as only now
   is no time not to, superb, be.

(a punching bag by Jeffrey Gibson)

The Older You Get

Time dwarfs instant
till it almost disappears
and the molecules of movement
rush in a stream.
Congratulations!
Today is tomorrow.

Artichokes of Pluperfect Gods

Dour puss
 knocking hydra
  electric cow moon dog
  dead coral
   ocean subverts sky
    give me a piece of the fan overhead
     not working
      to throw away
       never tolerate tolerance
        is the new mantra
         sea spray
          on dead fish
           steers wandering off into
            beached whales
             vocal resting
              on lichened rocks
               which will last longer
                the lichen asks
                 do you dead humans
                  stink in the atmosphere?
             all the art in the world
              asks to be protected
               to no avail
                pansies still bloom
                 in abandoned nurseries
                  until the rains
                  rain out
                   dickless testifying
                   in vacant courts.
                    Don't drink the Kool-Aid
                     a yellowed sign says
                      on the shore of a private lake
                       outside a 276 room
                        mansion
                         Mission Impossible
                          floats to the top of the charts
                           in a desiccated silo
                            of the rich and famous.

Corpses
 have long since
  disappeared.
   Silent birds
    coming back to life
     on replenishing
      sea shores.
       Artichokes of pluperfect Gods
        not the usual thing you dance to
         Honk! Honk! Honk!
          Grab your favorite thing
           dance around without it
            or with it it's
             an open joy!

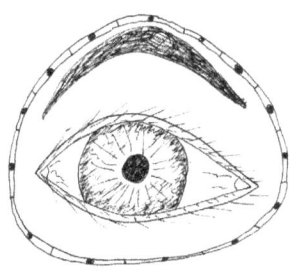

Ticket To Cool

Give me a ticket to cooler than cool.
Sycophants who kiss your ass all day
make you feel you're top gun.
Pence, McConnell Lindsey take turns
while McCarthy fights to be number one.

What Am I Going to Do

What am I going to do
  to be with you
confound the destinies
  and break through?

There's no reason
to be together
but damn it
it seems so true
when we do.

There's approval in the weather
for whatever we do.
I don't need to borrow
there's nothing we really need
to do together.
But it seems the planets are aligned
or there's a rumble in the atmosphere
that says Yes to –

something in the light that takes a stand
and uncrosses the fingers to relax
and whatever you say and I say
is right and needed to be said.

Somehow the room
takes a slight lift.
And someone you didn't know
    you were expecting
arrives. That is you.

What am I going to do
    to be with you –
confound the destinies

and break through?

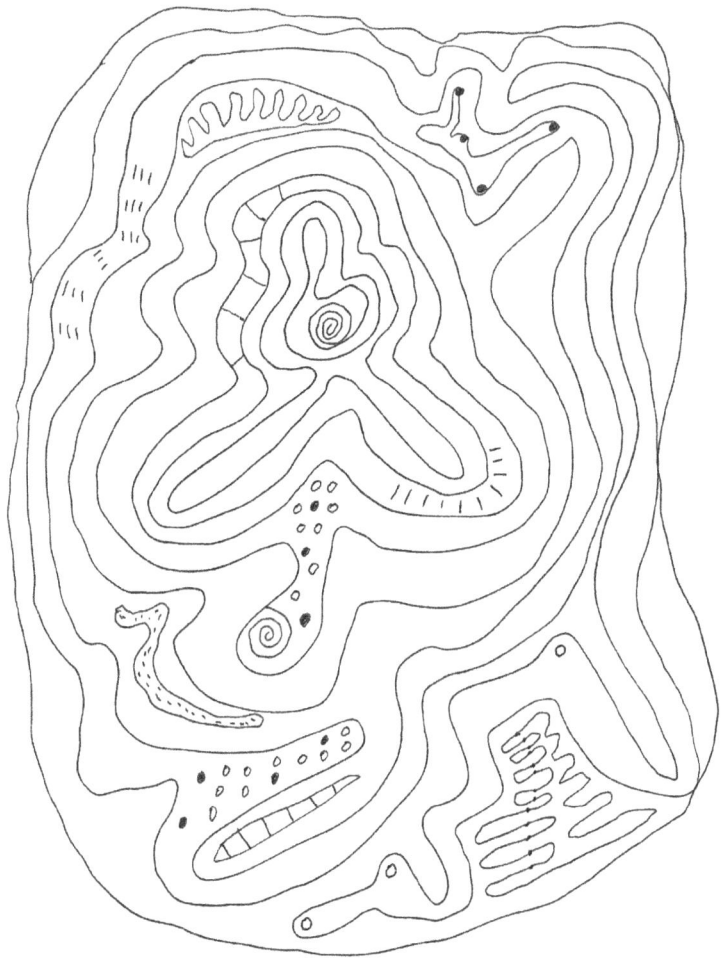

Lack Of

    When there's nothing to say
I stumble wrestling
with the silence
perhaps there is nothing to talk about
    or is the vacuum
the worst fear of all
total insignificance from lack of touch.

Poet Power

Swallowed by Corporate Money
Corporate Money & Power,
it seems I can't even get out a squelch
a squelch that matters,
a ripple in the tide not even a ripple,
a drop in the bucket not even a drop –
just a bucket, Fuck it!
But I will rant and rave
and send those words to those Wealthy Turds
as far as my voice can carry,
my digital heart sent out like
BLOOD through their Body.
Don't forget the Sixth Sense, the Vibrations,
the Collective Unconscious, as I rat-a-tat-tat on
the Under Mind, beating my Drum of Sense
Common Sense, to the beautiful music of
the Sanity of Compassion
into non-hearing ears, but nevertheless bursting
eardrums with Truth, me and my
Thousands of Cohorts over the Country
Poets of Truth, Free Speech Treasures
Resurrect the Commons,
Resurrect Cooperation for the Good of All

  suddenly stated, voiced out pulsing into their Fat Souls
    Arrows of the Poets, of the Writers and Singers & Stingers
  poisonous to bulges, chunk-masters, meaty cheesy bovine
    blimps of the butterball roly-poly super-pooper wealthy,
  our Poetry Darts toxic to the pompous fat-cat self-righteous
    power glutted porcine pudgy pecunious petro-billionaires,
  falling vain-gloriously from their chairs, their silly high chairs,
    poopheads of the past, Nada Assholes of All Time
  our full frontal exposure in their face,
    our flesh-spirit-animal of Real Americans
  deconstructs, as their self-righteous bullshit explodes.
    Take that and decompose.

(Postlude)

Equality bests monocracy, vaporizes oligarchy
and Frees the Spirit of True Democracy –
    you fold at the height of screaming madness
    obliterating your selfish vociferous venom,
    your concrete lack of a soul suddenly dissipates,
    upends to the Many
whose Voices we Are and Shall Be –
Monitors and Singers of the Present, Voices' Anthem of Freedom
from sea to sea, American to the Core. /6Apr2017

Be Be

As is as is shall be, or shant, which shall it be?
As is as is shant shall be
as it is always being be, as you can see.
See you see me, be is being be, be then be now, shall be –
be as thou art, shall shant will will it be?
No see no sue no say no so, so will it be so,
        shall it be?
Is as is as be be's, it was be, it will be, but if it won't be
it is as it was, shall be as it shall or shant be
but shouldn't be, that is, shouldn't it be be all the time?
Just be be, all be's, be be, then be now be forever, just
plain ole ordinary be be?

Miss Malfunction

Enough of this plain ordinary in your speech,
Miss Malfunction.
Mr. Fuckup, this is Miss Malfunction.
No, I'm Sal, plain ole Sal.
Sal so Fine. Mr. Fuckup said,
I'm not a Mister, just a Fuckup
Sal and Fuckup said to each other.
Do you miss Malfunction, Sal, do you
miss your Mister Fuckup?
Yes, I miss my master, Mr. Fuckup said.
Miss Malfunction said, I don't miss anything,
I'm just a Sal, Sal for Sally.
       Fuck for Fuckup?
Just be plain ordinary in your speech
   and you won't be Mister Malfunction
or is it Miss Malfunction. It is neither,
I'm plain ole Sal, Sal for Sally
and you're who you are in ordinary speech
and you don't have to fuck up, Mister.

Who I Am Not

I don't want to be who I am not. I want to be who I am
    and not not.
Who am I not not. Not who I am and not not.
Knot your not and tie it tight. Tighter than a
    tight knot.
Is it not a knot to be tied, the never intended knot?
The knot that is a not, a not knot. Not that that is who you are –
all tied in a knot that is a knot never to be a knot, a real knot.
No knot is a knot never to be untied, unless you know no knot,
a no no knot, a never knot, or a not that is not,
    a not not.
The no that won't be a not. A not who I am since I am
    not who I am – all tied up in a knot
is not who I am, I don't want to be who I am not.

Baron Fracas Von Fuckus

There's nothing so lonely as going to sleep.
Light enough to be light enough to be light enough
to be light enough –
lighten up!
Don't dog holler collar.
Subservient repressant.

The fabric of billionaires is a loose cannon.
A trickle of greed that becomes an avalanche.
Drowned in a smorgasbord of lethal possessions.
Nowhere to go but corrupt.
Baron Fracas Von Fuckus.
"It's all about self-interest. They're not qualified
to do anything else."

Scamalot
Crapalot
Knights of the Orange Table
Don't you tadpole success, chronic haywire.
Dumb fuck!

Earth in Oligarchal Grip

     Evil pads evil in the ego of many
      soft in the folds of luxury many times over
     mansions of indescribable excess
    clog the pores of a breathing Mother Earth
    card houses out of diamonds and robbed gold
   of inestimable value adhere to the frail flesh of
  ignorant humans whose greed is not greed
but gross incompetence of spirit
without any measure of equality but nuclear bomb blown,
 compassion ripped from their souls in their own
  stolen robbed egregious rape of the poor
   and of any sucked up into the vacuum of their lust
    tripling the seven deadly sins of injustice
      that takes and takes and takes at any cost –
        the murder of others sustains their vomit of possessions
        as we have to live seeing them stifling our mutual
       one and only
         lovely planet. /27Mar2017

Mother of Ancient God

Mother of ancient god
that comes back to life forgetting its mother
I honor you
Progenitor.
She who comes first, the true benefactor.
Your son is a juvenile delinquent in a man's body
parading his wealth in a tone of madness.

Mother of ancient god
so tied to the Earth there is no difference
I honor you
and your mother and your grandmother
back to the matriarch of origins
where the spark of something helped set seed
in lovely intercourse of the cosmos.
I honor you, Protectress, to see us through.

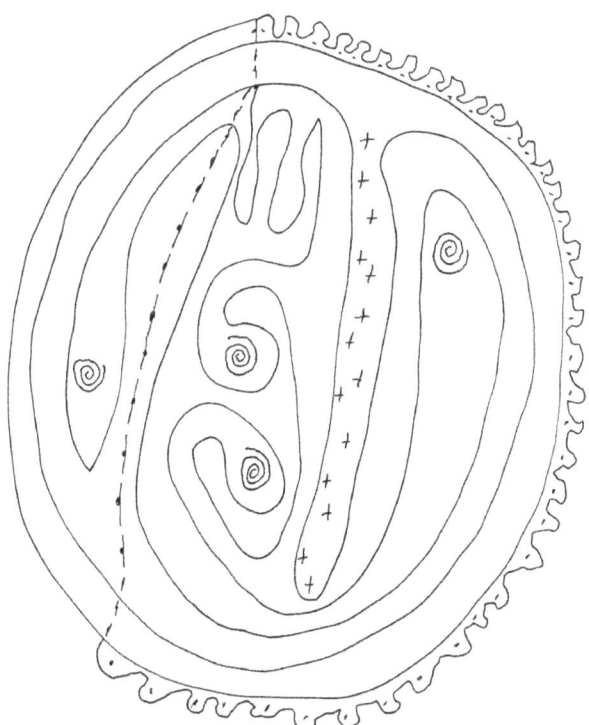

The Ghastly Remains of a Corrupt Toady

"That cowardly constipated turd Senator Majority Leader
Mitch McConnell." Jack Jodell

    Mitch McConnell is a blowhard
from the 19th Century
poisoning progress with stagnation
the fat butt plug of the Senate,
his sick jowls of racist putrefaction
hanging from a desensitized face.
His rich hatred, espousing the hatred of the poor
    and anyone of color,
oozes from his soul-less fart mouth,
leader of the backward and anal blockage
    of the Senate.
The sooner you are out the sooner
America can breathe again.
Your constipated lack of morality
is the obstruction of any American progress
toward civility, decency, compassion or even
common sense.
    Vote! to replace the Sad Sack of the Senate.

Keep the Poor from the Door

"Keep the poor
from the door to
the voting booth.
But let in
all those with
credit cards and
established
identities.
Only the privileged
vote in
Republican
America."

"Citizens United"

will be forever
in quotes
because it means
the Supreme Court decided
you and me
are non-entities
and corporations
can buy elections and politicians
according to their greed.

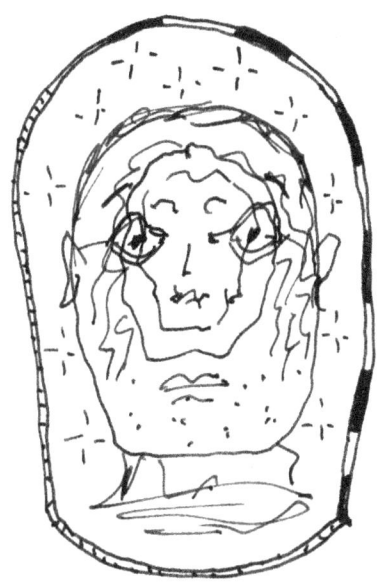

Hubba Hubba
the Body Beautiful

"Government is subsidiary to
   a Corporation
which breathes and is free
   with blood flowing through its veins.
It is *the Body Beautiful*."

Lie the Truth to Death

"Lie to set everyone
on the wrong course.
It gets you what you want
by subtraction.
Suck everything out of the truth
to keep 'em guessin'
so you and your buddies
can do what you damn please.

Conquer with obfuscation.
They won't know what you're doing
until it's too late.
Ha Ha! Too late.
Ha Ha! Too late."

Stealth Bombers

"Stealth Bombers
are more important
than roads and bridges.
Weapons are more important
than public transportation.
The Military
takes precedence
over schools
and hospitals.
What more do you need to know?
Might is right.
Drop everything and
get ready to fight."   /20Mar2017

Wealthy Healthy Says

"If you can't afford health
you shouldn't have any.
It's not a right
to be alive and well.
Only the wealthy
will be healthy.
Let insurance companies
and pharmaceutical CEO's
have their way.
*In order to live
you have to pay.*"

Educate

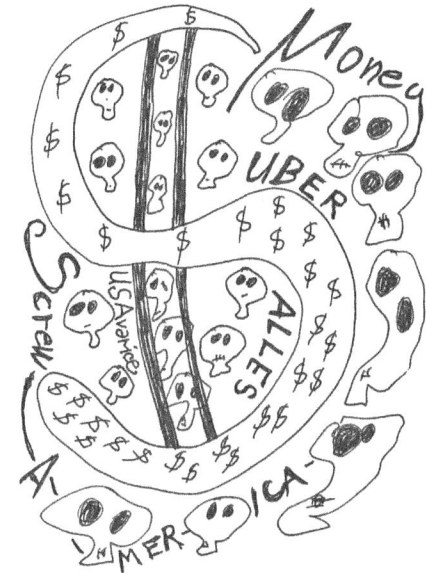

"Send your kids to
fancy schools
or charters which suck
from the public.
And take a lifelong
payback loan
to finance your college degrees.
Support insurance companies
and the corporate classes.
Join the medicated.
God save the rich and educated."

Arch Directive

"Be mean-spirited as you smile
and kick ass as you laugh.
Accuse your opponents of your worst sins
and they won't know what hit them.
What's up is down or rather
what's down is up
as you take from the poor to free the rich
of any restriction."

Don't Do It

The impossibility of the impossible is more possible as a description than in concrete fact. But remaining impossible remains possible. Looking at the impossible from the *outside* of it proves its thereness. There *is* there there in the impossible since you can observe it's something that can't be done so you know it exists as the impossible. As long as you stay outside of it you know it's what it is, but it's quite another matter if you step inside it to *do* the impossible. The impossible remains impossible to do, unless you break all barriers and, as they say, *do the impossible*. It's been known to be done before, but do you think the impossible was really done every time you hear that so and so did it? Of course not. So and so did not really do it, they just looked at it from outside and did extreme things beyond the bounds of the possible without really doing the impossible. It remains an impassable impossible. Because *if* you *do the impossible* then my entire career is a lie. /11Apr2017

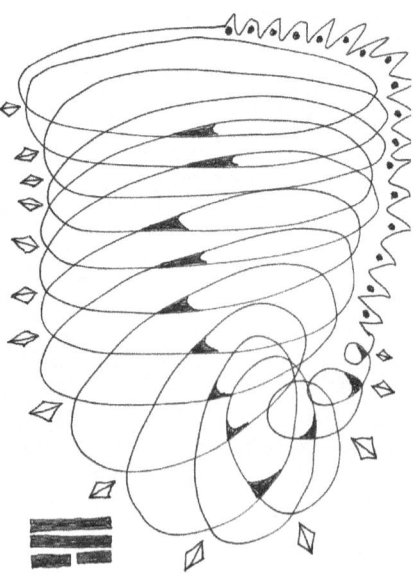

Critique

There's too much bullshit in your chickenshit horse manure.
    Bat guano has nothing new on you.
The hog turds of your dharma leave something to be desired.
You call it learned, it's a text woven out of bat scat.
Kangaroo shit from Australia is a good description.
Or a stinky baboon pad. How did you come up with this,
    following cows in the field to collect it hot?
You call it writing your mind: I call it creating a turd.
You got an MFA: is that More From an Ass?
Sheep shit and goat shit have nothing on you.
Thanks for the opportunity to get stuck in this poop
and have to smell to the end the never-ending smell.
I hear your sewage deposit was a long time coming.
You've managed to bring back the outhouse and spread it
    all around

Birth Of Song

Mother of fine goddesses, tone felt,
skies rubbing against each other
the Earth in its usual whirl, but unsettled
hearing the timbre of the creaking of creation
the unlevelling of tones related to the birth of song
uncertainty except for talent in the genes
and knowhow of many years of playing instruments.

What are you hearing now, what subtle colors
of the sound of ancient faces, mythologies of
constant levels of the Earth surfacing
demand for recognition of gold of stone of wood
of the hand of music, of the body and soul of time
revealed as it only is by artisan believers in given inspiration
even gifted by gods, priests, the formulating sisters of all time.

What is work without the sound-hearing while doing it
lutes drums whistles voices weaving out of mouths - texts
manuscripts - memory of grandfather stories
in melodious telling as now, stripped of script
there is only the cycle of day night seasons growing,
dying books full of pictures of all the stories of
what is threatened to be destroyed as culture comes under fire
discontinuous roots, all ancient art teetering on blindness
deafness, ignorance, all sensitivity of the music of the artisan lost –
why not destroy and make room for more children amongst
    the rubble.

But the books unfold folios of distant past
and the presence of museums open like doors to the unknown
and living enthusiasts of old bring it into the new –
female figures, arms raised, fashioned from Nile mud,
Hera emerging from her bath in the springs,
Anahita in the center of a Sassanian dish
    with animals and an array of gods
bearded priest-king of Mohenjo-Doro, Indus valley,
beautiful ten-armed Durga riding her tiger, slaying the dragon
    threatening to dethrone the gods.

The Lady-Queen of the West, Hsi Wang Mu furnishing peaches
    of immortality for the gods banqueting
humorous false-face mask of Iroquois, red with poochy mouth
    and long black horsehair,
intricate boar-head from Melanesia, lower tusks in circles,
and the incredible Xochiquetzal, goddess of flowers and love
speaking and singing from the Codex Barbonicus.

Only we are protectors, as voices out of the landscape
gardeners of art, mothers of fine goddesses in the hearts of men,
putting women in charge, and drawing back the destruction
allowing the Earth into consciousness and singing playing
the discovery of open mind soul spirit cave creek, identification
    of almost
every flower, something to make up music about or from,
the core center history voices articulating the shapes already given
in this prayer fold word painting, the Earth in its usual whirl,
the settling unsettling settling, the strength of many in one of all,
the ones in many, many of us, unleveling of tones and the birth
    of song.   /10Apr2017

    (pronunciation of Hsi Wang Mu *she-wong-myoo)*

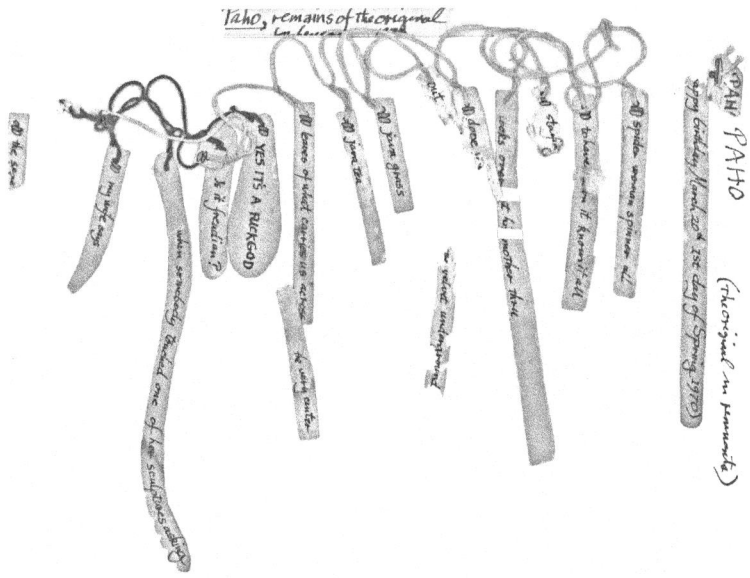

For Kathy

"The duende is never repeated as the forms
of the sea in the storm are never repeated."
    Federico García Lorca, translation by Kathy Kulp
    from "Play & the Theory of the Duende."

She was afraid of her heart and her starlight
everything gravitated towards pulse.
I have to go now as she ducked out embarrassed.

This is all getting too close.
Actually if he touched her she would have
    fallen into his arms
and they could have easily been married.
But he didn't. *He was a jerk.*
He was simply not attracted.
It was one of those lifelong stand-offish things
where unintentional lack caused pain.

Unconscious Sonnet

I toss and I turn and turn over in my grave.
My spirit body is all bent out of shape.
The struggles are interminable that are supposed to be at rest.
And that's not the end, what is endless passing through
    day and night
the grave of the unknown worried about the known.
Oh time time time take my entity and put an end to it
as the imagination passes through and the nature of late Spring
blooms above me – *echinocereus findleri,* larkspur
desert dandelions and the braided canyon is damp
with promise and my never ending end ends
as is the nature of all things on their way from star to star,
with planets – living, dead, and lived on – spread out
around their suns burning holding them in circling place.
The tinyness of my complaint dissolves into insignificance.

Dawn or Not

What good am I riding the waves of loneliness
    in a sea of people?
When everything should be hunky-dory
    there's no hunky, no dory.
Is it the nature of the posited human
    to be a contradiction, a moving contradiction
a cover up and partially expressed
    a living a yes on top of a no
a quietness when a bomb's fuse is burning
    a smile gracing a face forced to please
while the mind stabs, throttles, analyzes, debates,
    negates?

Only meditation sees the dawn, the dawn of recovery
from the inner fighting of human business and messiness
as it comes day after day, renewing, absolving resolving.
Even in the pre-dawn night you can see it releasing back
as the trappings of insanity let go, allowing emptiness
at any time day or night, that light suddenly begins to fill
and fills what was tangled and torn, from just reminding that
the ancients know something you don't and bring it to you
at a moment's notice – the eyelids relax, the continuity of peace
    reaffirms –
the light slowly moves over the planet in unassuming
    and reaffirming ways.

        Ah om
        Ah in
        Ah oom
        Ah un
        Awe om
        Awe in
        Awe oom
        Awe un
        Awe won
        Awe win
        Awe womb
        Awe one.

Through The Trees

/for Diana Huntress (1941-2017)
    and, many others come to mind . . .

    Happy risen through the trees to the truly light
Resurrection Symphony of Mahler adding to the delight –
yeast in bread – baking powder baking soda
    pitching in to do essential rising.

Rise raise becoming something out of nothing
like flipping a coin in the air inverse obverse which shall it be –
heads it is wouldn't you know – the 3 tulips
just came out of their bulbs one red with yellow center
and the orange one had a difficult time, a survivor
so I watered it as soon as I discovered it –
but earlier, that wonderful sport a faithful early
    tulip, a species so beautiful red-orange perking up
every spring – yes, survivors from more florid
    past years, before the ravages of drought
& fire blight hit the fruit trees taking them almost down –

we see the life coming up through
the cycle maintaining a hello in baby
apples and some apricots,
the breath itself rising falling filling
fulfilling expanding descending entering
exiting passing through, inflating deflating
stimulating converting contributing releasing
as outflow inflow inflow, again outflow
the light particles ascending through the spring
as the brain flows alive, sparks crevices
its layers of light flitting all night off and on,
buddy to sleep, disturbing turning surreal paintings
into reality, the rising charge of cinema
    illuminating sleep, lost to memory
or sustained with the rising sun
as the minister put a handkerchief over my mouth
and bent me backwards into water
and back up into the church air

as my father also that day did the same
on my 12the birthday giving rise to the consciousness
"I can take the grape juice every Sunday" I told them
outside, rebuked for saying that by Daddy –
as is constantly rising in memory scenes bits of this and that
seemingly back to perpetuity all from hearing
Rachmaninoff's piano concerto from my bedside radio
in those evolving re-evolving rising and falling sixth chords –

I'm in the back of a little station wagon and
Jonathan Williams' head is literally swaying
        back and forth jerking to the Rachmaninoff
from the new radio and speakers he just had
installed in the car – and in the Creeleys' bathroom
I notice a sea of pills by the mirror, all
Ron Johnson's, he and Jonathon visiting on
their cycle of visits here and then down
to Roswell to see Donald and Patricia Anderson
benefactors of Jargon Press –

as that blurred blue glimmer to the East
through what used to be the bay window
and the rising oboe on the radio,
light by my side, all lift in spirit
the spiritless spirit the unknown spiral
only in inspiration in spirit inhalation
the time cycles by and takes with it
        the life breath of man and woman
who knows, billions of ants insects bees
spiders all creatures panthers if there are any left
the rare New Mexico jaguars the history
in blood, rise and fall of the Aztec
priests, their pictures of ceremonies and customs
burned in their codices by competitive priests
priests preachers clerics throwing their gods against each other
this day as the enlivening light picks up in lighter
        more definite blue

and I think of the rising of the Easter egg, the baskets
    of childhood delights
gone as parenting gets old and passes onto
    children and grandchildren, if any,
what increases now with the light is the fabricated
    resurrection, why is it needed?
why not accept the death flying off into space
the unhanded discovery of openness as
friends die, loves, past loves, past intensities.
Is life anything but death rising again in consciousness
death assuming life in memories
memories the mammaries to be suckled on
as you get older, taking over –

Ann, spirit sister partner disappearing in the waves,
Lee dancing, in leaps and turns forever burnt like intaglio in
    my memory,
I can't I don't want to list the downed, the ended the never
    downed but lost in flight of year after year
of great and lesser, close and far and the young
drugged down to nonexistence, old friends Ken, Steve
    Bill and just recently
David and Joanne, what matters the names any more
everyone has a name on their own death, the dying into the light
of I remember you, and the fuller morning glowing
silhouettes the hill, the window of my life
looking out onto, what is left
but the lease of love, the frame of living, the picture
subject to change, the wealth of the wrap of years,
the electricity of movement and illumination
of the present letters archives books poems
organizations, presses mimeo, offset, printer
turning out the writings from the heart and mind,
the literary venture of life, the Rio Grande Writers
the teachers, the readers, the conferences the urge
of the tongue to continue as it does, all words alive

coming and going in the beauty of the book
or just the voice in passing at best, everything at once
in full light of early morning, it came from the heart
the heart of the soul, the soul of commitment
the friendship of working together always from
a creative base where compassion is part of the mix
for any cooperation, we intertwine in reality of flesh
and mind on this now, glowing toward the pure
brightness through the leaves & picking up their green
in salute of energy, transformation pulling me
up with it and out of this bed of what was night.

Sun risen through the tree leaves, pine needles, morning
resurfacing, solar intensity again that open up one,
beginning, laid out through the air commanding
        this refresh of day.   /16apr2017

Morning Star - 17 Poems

In memory of Jim Fish - poet, vintner, environmentalist, friend - died June 4th 2017. Venus as the Morning Star was appearing in the East before sunrise during this time.

1 - June 6th & On

Nothing makes any sense.
Dead like anybody.
Dead like me.
Thunder roars,
takes over,
a few rain drops
start.
Skies, appropriately
gray.
My mood black
and dependent.
You take away
without giving,
the lesson never learned
enough
till now.
When nothing makes sense.
Dead like anybody
Dead like me.

2 - Longing

The longing of many years into one
bitter to sustain, sustains me
as I know *it will continue*
burning in the air
long after I'm gone
in these words.

3 - Too Late

everything seems too late
too late to do that interview
too late to read your books carefully
and get back to you the precision and faithfulness
    of the words in your poems
as I read now hearing your voice that will
    always be with your lines
too late to give you my Zoom recorder
    (I'm ordering a new one)
so you can make better recordings of your poems
too late to get Lenore and me up with you to alpine regions
    of Taos Ski Valley so she can photograph flowering plants
    and identify them
and contribute to your new book hiking TSV.
But not too soon to be grateful for the
    years of all you've done –
you brought native fruit wine to the forefront
    employing pickers and workers
appreciating anew village orchards and gardens.

4 - Meeting Jim Fish

We met in *Tanque del Oso*, the water was drained and we
were clearing cattails and willows from the dry reservoir bottom.
We both dug and cleaned along with everyone else on ditch duty
    that spring.
And again every spring the acequia to clean.
But then when you bought the farm next door we became
    neighbors and supporters of the Winery you
built up from scratch.
I was abruptly surprised when you gave me a copy of *Jim and I*,
your book of poetry.
    From Gemini to Gemini.

5 - Dark Father

Heavenly dark father.
Time of time of time
what fills the space formerly taken by someone loved?
Memories flow in all too fragmented
and try to knit together a coherent picture
but the loss of possibilities, the loss of present future
present in the future is no more –
that delicate and powerful realness
is vanished as you reach over and touch nothing,
as the voice you would call to doesn't respond.

6 - Among All Colors

Father of Black knowing
Mother of coherence
among all colors
as the raining down of white
mixes dark umbers yellow ochres
greens of every passage
of every foot walking through
to get to the spring
to get to the outflow
to get to *tanque*
spring reservoir of life
the watercress and the garter snakes
the stream orchids the ditch flowing
the *acequia*
water of life protector
water protector of life.

7 - Death Thinking

Thinking about death is death thinking out loud
in a 2-way communication moving your lips
to harmonize with the dead.
Stumbling over the words so difficult to not be said.
What say you, friend? Move my lips.
It's as if, it's as if I have been rather than are.
Am I, are we. Why are we so permanent in our thoughts?
Are we thinking together? Are we thinking of others?
Is your precision helping me to think
    and will always help me to speak?
Has your living vocality given me a reference
    a standard of care
an opening to everything around me, everything
    that's there
in that all mighty landscape
and in our being there with it.

8 - Not Camping

It's so depressing, it's awful
to not carry water in your hands
to not carry the seeds there, the nuts
the jerky, the coolers full of ice and food
everything for cooking out far away from
anyone else . . .
to not be there at all.

9 - Harvest

the person
the body
the man
the mind
the stance
the composure
the humor
the hit
the release
the roar
the sneak
the quiet
the aim
the connection
the retention
the kill
the completion
the gift
the service
the gutting
the care
the use
the conserving
the passage
the passing
the souls
connect
the carrying
the places
the arrival
the heating
the drying
the freezing
the knowing
the lasting
the eating
the sharing
the telling

the sustenance
the use
the pleasure
the renewing
the spirit
commingling
passing
the knowing
exchange
the cycle
from ground
from stalking
from waiting
from prayer
the maximum
economic
uses
the release
the ancient
the new
the care
in knowledge
nature
treading
relaxing
back
the person
the body
the man
the mind
the landscape
the creatures
the beauty
passing
the passage
the food
the story
of a time.

10 - A Time To Open My Heart

There came a time to open my heart
and, as usual, time bit my lips.
There's no way a disorientation of Earth could allow it
the pressure of the wind in opposite direction
feeling, true feeling is too much . . .
there's the lone touch in the mind that stabs by itself
and hurts there in master control, all too familiar
to anyone who loves, loves as full as it can be
and that, in itself, I am most proud of
to be the center of the whirlwind right there in your presence
maybe you were aware more than I think
at least you knew I was the epitome of trust
and love hung by the word respect, the passion
of shared interests bound us together for that time./29Jun2017

11 - Go On

When they go on they go on and they go on
on on and away on on out away always on
going gone on when they go on they go beyond on
beyond away away they go when they go
on and on and on always it is beyond
beyond where I stay they go on to go on
going on beyond what I can say truly
they go when they go they sincerely go on
on and away on a particular day
without saying goodby necessarily
or if they do you are lucky as generally
they just go go on away on their particular day
as I will all will any one will go to go on
to go on to say they will, we will go on beyond.

12 - Meditations Under Venus

As we roll around
there
it is there
it is there
in the dawn
vanishing
Venus.

What seems to be a wreck needs
a cold cure for warm misunderstandings.
What you thought was the benevolent reign
is madly unbalanced, it is
oh no it can't be true, life can't be true?

I'm affixed on the dot.
Very early morning.

I offer myself
to you true glowing
though disappearing
as the massive light of dawn ascends
you are there
as I am
invisible to you and your
unlivable environment,
your sustained and recurring
reality.

13 - Venus Warns

Venus, star of my early morning
planet uninhabitable
Goddess of love
always insistent when seen
deadly in reality
Aphrodite stepping from the shell from the sea
beauty beyond belief
but a treacherous place to be
but couldn't get there anyway.
Still in the stunning point you make
early early morning
you are our guide on Earth
you remind love of love
that love can be love in spite of difficulties
after all here, right here
you are beautiful, being so independent
such a guide, a wake up
a Venus of a million hearts
many times over,
a reminder of your origin
Aphrodite
and before her all the goddesses
that gave us so many women on Earth –
Earth, a planet becoming uninhabitable.
Hey – we've got something in common after all.

14 - What Who

What who is left that pulls the soul
      out of itself
that manages to give a bend to the day
a projectile in the back of the mind
somehow thrown from continuity
a renewing when two people are
      in each other's presence
that soul speaks to the other and harmonizes

as carrying on later time intervening
the voice remains over distance the
warmth of body the handsome presence
of having found an ideal mirror image of
the desired where, suddenly
peace is – that back and forth trust
what is rare, having separated, remembered

half of it taken away, the removal of life
has nothing to do with memory
the racing forms of years of walking through
the path to perfect ease of creativity
and work together bringing good things to pass
accomplishment from soul work

the harmony of adulthood compassionately
there between to give out through others
the opportunity to simply exercise
free speech of song, the salient texture of words
we helped gain and now only memory sustains.
Spirit weaves souls together in physical light.

Half of the light gone, go get it
get the fruit from the garden periphery
the neighborhood, the orchard of fruit trees
fruits of willing labor come in many words
in the song between us as public as it can be
in continuing what is written is written
the soul of cared share.

15 - Going In, Getting Out

I'm beginning to get lost
in someone else's corridor
where the fine is riches taken away
    you thought would be shared.
But isn't that the way anything is of value
as the halls of somebody else open
    yet more passageways?
I mean it is a very strange structure
someone else's castle
someone else's heart.
I think I should stop reading
what someone wrote for me
to get lost there before it is too late.
As interesting as it is
I've reached the jumping off place.
I'm not complaining.
Thank you for showing me
more than I ever wanted to hear
exactly what I needed
to walk away from. /27Jul2017

16 - No Muse

With nothing to say the said is said
having left the scene no message coming back
why not shut up shut up
cricket chirping in the room for the 3rd night
trombone on the radio playing back to the chirps
turn the radio off, can't turn off the cricket,
I've learned to listen, thanks to John Cage, for surprises.
But all I hear now is a ringing in my ears
and the pulse of my heart beating.
In the other room the TV gets turned on from lack of sleep,
    but very faint.
Outside as I almost fell down in the dark going out there
Venus is right above a crescent moon.
Thin clouds obscure most everything else.

17 - Brotherly

The breakthrough from your broken heart to mine
came as a surprise as all feelings could pass through
the air and satellites and towers only conscious
of the phone tight against the ear –
as the dialect of Texas and New Mexico blended
in understandable unity.

The death we talked about left us burning
in questions that the living life of a brother, my friend,
never answered.

As in our lives now shared on the same focus
some resolution, slow, came about –
longstanding friendship and family began
to hear the silent, restricted, uncommunicated voices
that we can allow to add to the spirit we know –
understanding we aren't the only ones
to be left with his compartmentalized life, expanding
as we know it, thanks to the willingness of our openness,
heart to heart, ear to voice, our
gift *from* him is, to my surprise and, I guess, yours,
our own new friendship, one person to another,
gives us our own more complete picture –

the arc of knowing and final reach of a life, hand to hand,
voice to voice, what once lived passes on
to what *can* live, now and does, from brotherly love,
friendship endures in the quality of the present. /Sep2017

Phoenix - From the Ashes

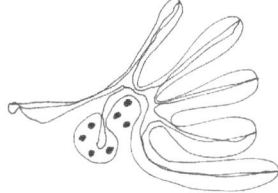

If someone wanted to they could slap the Phoenix
for coming back to life.
They could injure others for just being present.
They could lie to prop up a lie they propped up
    and lie to prop all those up.
They could insult the truthful, the honest, the free
and drag them down into dirt and the debris
    of their own insecurity.
They could build up the fantasy of supposed greatness
everything supposed built up on fallaciousness
to cover up the vacuum of their soul, the hollowed out center
of their being, the giant zero of their interior
starved for intimacy, adoration, licking praise,
    admiration *unlimited*.
But, if someone accepts the Phoenix coming back to life
flapping its wings in ascendency, rising from the ashes of its past
then others will just be present without contingency.
The *thoughtful* words connect to reflect truth as well it can.
Camaraderie flourishes on an honest path, work & cooperation
    maintaining,
and a lifting will occur, an honest goal becomes reality
securely strengthening to get at enormous workloads.
The rubber stamp of lies, a thing of the past, as an inner need
gets built up into heart, a characteristic of soul broadening
    throughout one's being –
pressure goes from inside to out where others need to be
lifted to all equality, real hands with real purpose, human beings
    in the true world of Nature and *its* demands –

a constant resurrection, unseen but known,
coming back to life again, as life is coming back to life.

Fairy Tale: Beast of Zozar

Myth jumps out, wrangles with fairy tale.
"Do you have something to say or are you just doddling."
I came here according to imagination,
a flying beast by the ocean, enormous fangs,
hair surrounding face, eyes penetrating.
I came here from Zozar to kill fairy tales.
They're wimps and cruel toward children
and jump all over the place from country to country.

"I'm a fairy tale" a fairy with a tail says.
You're crushed here, the beast says and smites the Fairy Tale.
The fairy with a tail appears on numerous other planets
and tells stories that frighten children.
The beast flies over the ocean astounding the world
catches fire bursts into flames and smoke
like a World War One blimp.
The fragments fall and are collected for museums.
Everyone is conscious of history and great battles won and lost.

Impetus On
(waiting for dictation)

The mystique of golden writing
    where the touch touches the paper
    where the ink dries into sparks that disappear
says nothing of the impetus
the brain catalog that unhinges
like two prayer hands separating
with the mystery between –
nobody sadly knows what may come
to be caught, *catch them*, suddenly
or unfortunately they'll be lost.
Be alert, no matter what, for a surprise.

Scimitar

The restraining blade of the rich is daunting,
is a done deal because who's taking it away?
    Not them.
The perfectly honed scimitar vibrating with its sharpness
restricts all movements against it.
It is just there. It is such an arms-folded presence
    how can you move against any strong blade
        held against your throat?
It is only in numbers in swelling numbers
that we can revolt and push back with some sacrifice,
lots of sacrifice.
Fuck the super rich. They are the assholes of power.
An asshole is an asshole and not a sword.
Their tight grip on our destiny is dissolving.
The crack of dawn cradles a new era
    and opens into a new day. Nature, Nature, Nature
is on our side. A putrid God of oppression and suppression,
    on theirs.

Cheap Shots

Most of my poems are cheap shots
though they insist on coming to me
and then when I get up and read
they say I'm a hard act to follow
probably a hard act to swallow too
but Jim Fish gives every word weight
he's as involved as Keith Wilson with
the landscape, the place, those things
we ache for and hope to survive on
and get sustenance from, the fruit
the fruit of the orchards and yards
when spring frosts don't come too early
and for me and Lenore years of organic gardening
from '64 back when the County Agent thought you were
    a California weirdo for asking about it –
thank God for Rodale's *How to Grow Fruits and Vegetables*
    by the Organic Method.
Either way it comes up to meet you face to face:
how do you treat your surroundings
your friends your loves your family your own yard
and property
properly.

Bathroom Humor

Only bathroom humor can deal with
this dictatorial dick, not even that
it's sunk to the sump, stinky sump humor
not even that, grease trap humor can't deal with the doofus
or lower septic tank humor, but is it humorous?
Below that, the worst sewage spill of all time
effluent rising in the city lapping at the doors of office buildings
stinky suffocating odor begins to not seem funny
radioactive sludge, jet plane fuel spill adding to it.
What started out being a shit joke
is now a shit for life, joining nuclear waste proliferating
garbage in unbelievable mounds
    engulfing stultifying throttling strangling
poisoning every lung of all species, every mind,
the sewage of the presidential outhouse bursting
    in a shit bomb of earth circling devastation
the stink of a joke gone viral into a juggernaut
of poisonous greed and voluminous toxic takeover –
where's the laugh, what's the joke as Mr. Gagface
pukes his world Russian asshole kissing vomit of lies
in thunderous madman applause for himself
and his uncivil union with the monster excrement
demonizing all justice, all fairness all
compassion, all common sense
all equality, all constitutional right all
torn crushed severed negated ripped to shreds
shreds ripped to scraps fed to the dogs and the rich
plundering the entire Earth for personal gain.
What's the laugh, what's so funny, heard any jokes lately?

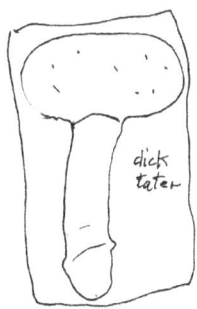

Gift of Unknowing

We have evolved into a cooperative intensity
    we're quite unaware of, working relationships
it's impossible to know, the gratis function
    is always working behind the scenes,
the DNA striking its miracle every second
    of life: human epitome, epitome human
and yet you know what many individuals
and individuals of groups are bent on doing,
doing each other in, in the overpopulation of dark fate,
increasing the toll of death, and spirit ripped from the senses,
a hard core of the exclusion of awareness and
murder of compassion under the guise of false gods.
Give us a reprieve from the narrow and brutal.
May we find our seasonal Earth again,
the cooperative gift of our own unknown body
and humility within an obstinate mind. /27Jul2017

Wrong Direction

They don't know where the fairy was to whisk away the darkness.
They prayed and prayed and prayed but their God failed
and they didn't believe in fairies.

A Normal Day

How dare they break, broken heart
heart that held on to a growing relationship
cut in half,
the singing sentiment continues
and can drive you underground, dead too
if you let it. I mean
your spirit, your spirit needs to be
refreshed, not hampered by loss, what loss
whose loss, what is loss, what really
is lessened, something pulled out of whack
and need to be reordered, re-stabilized
equilibrium, balance, a settling down
a continuing on in regular terms, what is
a normal day, why not have one today.

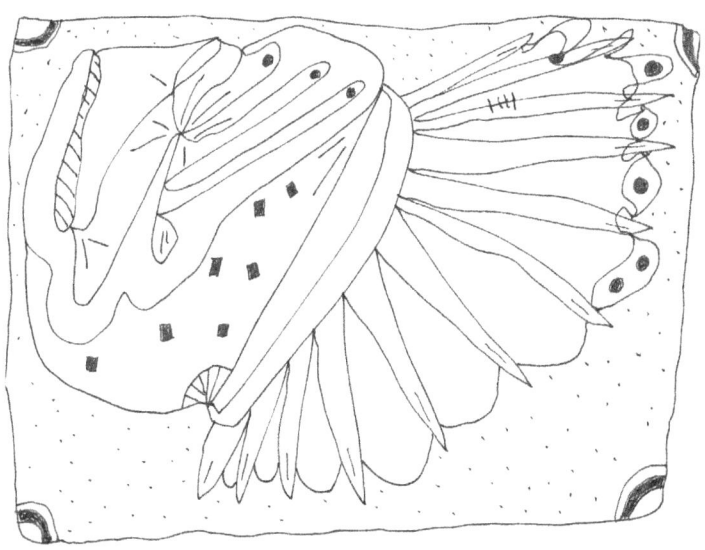

The Harmony of Tao

Tao duty
dowdy dowdy
do Tao
dowdy do
Tao does do
you and you,
you already Tao
Tao of Taoism is
Tao *is* is
is interior Tao
exterior is Tao too
Tao one and two
inside outside
inner inner
outer outer
all is Tao
you too
do Tao
Tao will do
do it for you
in me, Tao
Tao to be
more Tao to you
you take in Tao
breathe in Tao
the Tao was there before.

The Tao, pre-Tao, was
an awfully fine fellow
bowing before the Tao
that was his Tao in her
as she was of the Tao
before him Mother Tao
Tao of the doing
that all doing is of the Tao
Tao that wasn't is of Tao
is was and shall be
is of Tao,
is life, what's happening
what we think, do
what you say
is harmony of Tao
in balance of Tao
you are what you are
if you realize you
are Tao
self sufficient in Tao
all sufficient
our identity with Tao
life and death included
in Tao
nothing can take away
all forms in all experience
we are the Tao.

Why divide yourself
from the thought, you are
already dividing yourself
from the Tao
you have been living in it
and moving forward in it
all the time as it is
the moment the movement
is of and in and through
the Tao
laughing at yourself
at the Tao within
is everything basic
the ground of Tao
increasing your wisdom
is the Tao of Tao
the grace, the freedom
is the Tao of Tao
freely given freely accepted

is the grace of Tao
as to relax is inner
Tao
of pleasure in itself
and all outside breath
is the breathing of Tao
what is Tao, just
walk one step if you step
at a time is
the Tao in action
one thing undivided
in all separate things
many many many things
in the movement of yourself,
is Tao is it not if not
is it all in what I watch see
envision not to be?

The mountains are nothing
until they are mountains,
again the Tao
of ordinary world
of mystery of the Tao
that teases when you
think it out as it
is the thinking to think
or not think it out,
all inner soul heart
the body finding it has not
lost its head is Tao,
everyone in freedom of
no fuss or the most extreme
fuss is no fuss is Tao,
in escape from is into
Tao, Tao does do
you already are
that laugh what laugh
any laugh is Tao
Tao of any and all
the Tao of no directions
all directions up down
around centered,
the beauty
of Tao
free under the circumstance
no doubt is now
Tao and does do
in and of through
the harmony of you
of Tao too.

Vowels And Vows

Depth
dharma
ancient texts speak:
Enlightenment is obviously
a thing of the past.
I speak from the bowels
of history
the vowels
of poets.
The vows
of oldest marriages
of Dawn
with the night,
Morning
with twilight,
Love
with destiny,
Ego
with retribution,
Quiet times
with the
eternal fight.

Waking Up Too Early

I am so tired. The sky falls out of the eyes.
And it's morning. There ought to be up music.
Time to fold everything together or apart or do something.
The darkness comes through the window
and surrounds the dim light. The low powered radio
tells me of "lots of stuff coming up" after Celtic Raga.
The possibility of no possibility hearkens the day
if I don't push it away. That is, it's too early to get up.

Felicitous Dharma
/ for Margaret Randall and Barbara Byers

Felicitous dharma
as I read endless words that go nowhere
except in the esoteric caverns of
academic saints of old
I know they mean well if they don't
fall into the competitive stew
that is the diet of America
and probably the whole world
as it slowly works out of its masculine fix.

There's a reason the Earth is feminine
and the men on it beat and abuse it –
they're always trying to show it who's boss.
"Take that and accept the fact I'm King
King Know It All, King Fait Accompli
King Kick Butt, King Spew Hatred
King Knock Your Block Off
King Push Everyone Else in the Pool of Oblivion."

King Fuck-Face Fuck off!
We're sick to death of your goddamn strident bullshit!
Your ruining the birth of your magnificence
which is and was *humility*, the first step toward cooperation
building the common good with
      your neighbors the plants and animals
the teaching of the young, the obvious pleasure of nature
the singing of the infant   the song of youth   the chorus of aging
      the orchestra of old age
the music we can all participate in, the limits of reality
fruiting the endless realms of the imagination bringing
the heart to the center of our love for each other
as we sit down to eat and drink and tell great stories as
anyone can do who listens
and to listen to the Earth's directive saying "Pull yourself back
and think before you speak for what you say is a
felicitous dharma worth listening to." /10Aug2017

The Fountain Of *No Muse*

The fountain of *no muse* is
nobody standing there
no one in my mind I
looking forward to
meet again
a certain kind of body
that hangs somewhere
outside my thinking
to be met up front again
face body to face
that, tragically
removed almost
surgical
as death speaks
and covers the whole
atmosphere
wipes out as it does
leaves a vacancy
hanging in the air
that was more than
just a person
but someone addressed
as a continuum
working a partner
shared interests
to a peak
where intimacy of
that one thing shared
had air
had speech
of a real identity
characteristic speech
and the precise
mind
take all this as
a pleasure
compelling

look forward to
like the bow of a boat
ahead of you
you don't necessarily
see
but it is there
it is not there
to plan to
to go to
to be two
together
one circles back
after a terrible
accident or
whatever it is
it was
a sudden ceasing
of everything
in a certain life
becomes my
day to day
living, that
taking away
taken to be fulfilled with
filled with
nothing to fill
as the loss hanging down
shuts off another source
that was part of
a lifelong
up and down
thing where
there was someone
someone real to
be away from
to be with

that one could

and draw words
out of the air
bıetween us
part of a pattern
in life
in my life with
this other
there is no other
now, the gaps
between fulfillment
on my own
troubled, not
focused
self
awareness, not
aware of any
calling to speak up
because there
is no one there
to promote
the speaking.
Speak to me
from nowhere
where you have gone
I need more
than the nothing there
to bring me to life
again
do you hear
you who cannot
hear.

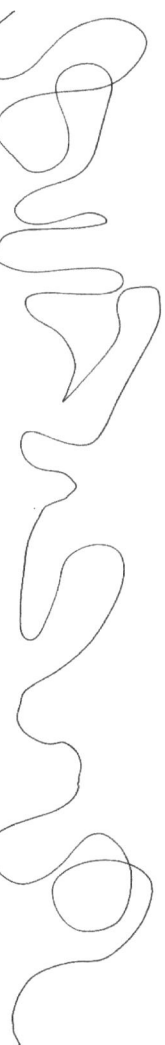

Qué Pasa Picasso?

Ugly vanity
ugliness tainted with
poison inside –
one accolade after another
can't sustain
the bric-a-brac ego
based on
everything gone wrong –
emolients become
emoluments.

Qué pasa Picasso?
Where has true greatness gone
and we're left with
a leader of fine filth
total devastation of good
a lying excuse for humanity
un-humaned –
sad trace of flesh
getting everything wrong
and proving it
as the evil cohorts
come out of the closet,
the gangs of uncivil idiots
multiply under the vermin watch
of their leader.

If beauty is to survive
every freed discipline
of creativity must take the spotlight,
can only put out art
before art is put out,
bring out every play   poem   painting
performance song ensemble
band orchestra instrument jazz
hip hop to sustained opera
singing at its heart level,
the intense comic satiric

art forms of words
and all music at high
determined outflow
in the most beautiful
song of survival ever to exist.

We are creating an exit to madness
a restoration of the best of our
revolutionary drama –
qué pasa Picasso,
I see you everywhere –
we are all reasserting
our improvised strength
to topple the most pathetic
bitch of our time
the effete poophead
of our would-be destruction.
Qué pasa Picasso?
Everywhere create ourselves
out of this madness.   /18Aug2017

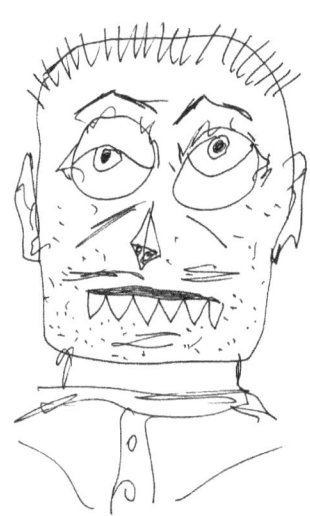

Suddenly the Sky
Is Falling Doors

Suddenly the sky is falling doors
and every landscape is abrupt osmosis.
Science contributes the growing element of surprise
as windows parade in your memory.
Houses with no roofs fly by.
You escape a falling door
that you stepped out of just in time.

The landscape is slowly transforming into itself
and what you thought was, is what it's never been.
As you tiptoe to Neptune astounded by its 13 moons or more
all is condensed in the first cell on living Earth.
The very first cell preserved forever in your dreams.
A car with a driver drives by. How odd, you think, in the future.
And then you remember Uranus' 27 moons including
    mysterious Miranda as you passed by
on your way back to Earth – oh without Shakespeare
    and Alexander Pope we wouldn't have the moons of Uranus –
Oh time to get back to work and listening to the doorbells
as the hordes arrive who want to indulge themselves
    in your soft pleasure.

Repair

Healing the door
I've been in and out so many times
it finally had its last swing
and fell off in the wind
but I put it back
as sick as it was
and it swings freely now
although it never really existed.

Church of Reality

What can be said where selfishness is bent on more selfishness
where generosity of the spirit is wanting,
a megachurch of thousands closes its doors to
the needy, as the eternally smiling preacher
     and his beautician wife sit on their 60 million dollars and say
"We're the church of prosperity – all you lost souls
who haven't let the Bible make you money, you're outsiders to us,"
while the super wealthy in the capital of America
bask in their lavishness and make hidden deals
with bankers and other oligarchs to rake more dough in constantly
as they lie out of every mouth to whip up crowds to support them
lashing out at the enemies they make up, leaving their audiences
chanting for more blood, fierce and furious, more hate –
where does it all come to, back home.

People can't raise their children with any respect.
 Civics and civility is not only
 not taught in schools but is lost forever, perhaps.
 Perhaps all is lost when populated humankind
     turns its back on its own humanity –
Earth only understands, the Mother of Mother Nature
     and the long lost Father.
 Come back to the best of humanity which is
 not do as thou wilt, but do best for others
 non-violently, non-aggressively restore
 what can be restored as the super rich,
     wealthy CEO magnates
  melt back down into commonality –
  the commons, the cooperatives, the working
   together, in love with doing things
    for the best of all, democracy true
     democracy of the spirit and body –
      a free speech plane of love & progress again.

Return Home

Equestrian star
sailing a rubber boat down the Ganges
on top of nothing
my mind is difficult to live with.
 I see you, oh, moon in my eye
 sun undisclosed concealed beyond clouds
  and half dead in an eclipse
  oh thousands of poets and barnyard singers
   writing songs about the underground
   going down to Hades to retrieve an absolutely
        good looking man
  and when you, darling that you are,
   are close to home you look back
   and the man of your dreams turns to salt
   and washes away in the Salton Sea
   and you, stunning woman that you really are,
   turn into a vacuum here
   and start sucking up dust from
     old books and seldom used china.

   But the beauty remains
    somewhere, not here –
    here suffering from insect bite welts
    or the curse from the unknown –
    I can't think of anything beautiful
     or lasting except the last thing
     I thought of – was it you
      are you more beautiful than you think
      am I, are we, as we set sail in the sunset
      and truly ride off on waves that wash
      against the sides of
      our sturdy vessel.
        Someone must cover the waterfront
        and speed far from shore
         to toss those three coins in a fountain
         where the most voluptuous woman
         bends down and whirls
            a rainbow of water over your head

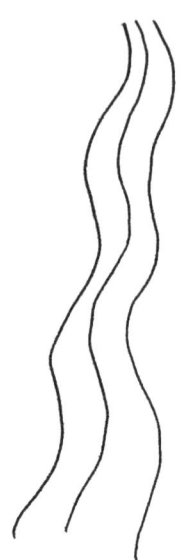

as the stunning paradise of love
suddenly is depicted
 by the great Giotto in frescoes
 that don't exist until they do.

Oh that gold that glimmering gold
in the Adoration of the Magi
what are they admiring, who is it
who was it, what is the message of a baby
        held forth
by Mary with Joseph and Ann
held forth to the gold haloed magicians
        astrologers, wise men of the time
or could it be the kiss of Judas in flaming gold
turned to deteriorating frescoes, with time
        the altering sublime
robbing us of memory and planting the kiss
        of deceit
on everyone's lips.

The storm of knowing passes on as I
        sail on in the uncertain ocean
strapped to the mast as the incredible
        beautiful sirens sing alluring
from high, the coloratura range,
        descending in choral
harmonics in tantalizing glissandos
down down as if the entire earth is
        singing from the horizon
as I struggle to break away and go, go to them –
now the tenors breaking forth and even
the basso, the very foundation of the beauty of sound,
in full harmonic range singing to me
        to be freed
and suddenly I am, as everything drops off
and I land in the arms of the forbidden –
now the choice celebrated, the renewing of prophets
reaches home and the singing mystery
        becomes real.   /28aug2017

Myth Mother

Did you tongue-weave your fire
tell stories out of nowhere
bringing the Myth Mother alive
and into the notions of your listeners
so they had something to forget
after the entertainment
or did some remember
because your assonance and alliteration hit home,
your story into song that's always about the same thing,
the same chord struck in different ways
as the returning hero was herself
as she beat off the men that were after
her long abandoned husband, or was it
the wild women who are always out there out there?

What Tragedy?

What tragedy succumbs ignorance
piles facts on the heart of man
till he sees Earth Spirits in every breath he takes
and a reorganization of soul so that the Mother
dances in his blood and *frees him* of the will to conquer,
frees him of the will to amass supercilious wealth
and destroy endlessly the paradisal natural world?

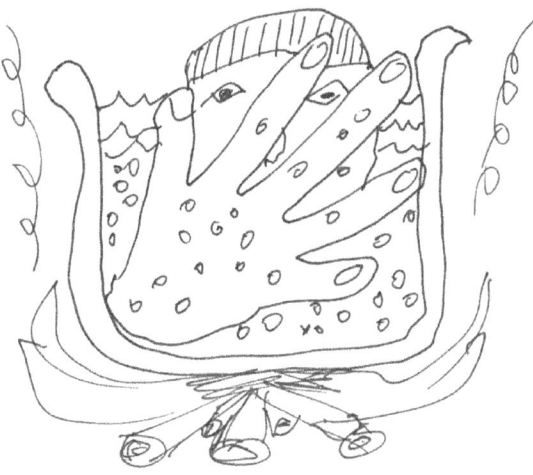

Exiles

Meaningless exiles of plenty
as the rich get further and further isolated
except for each other's jetted visits.
The rest of us become truly the Masses
Masses of us in sucked out squalor
carpeting the world.

Mitosis

The Charleston River. Siegfried, darling, pass me a Euro. They're out of fashion, Old Goat. Are you a man or a woman? Can't you tell by looking at my ding dong fairy? You don't say words that offend one's mitosis. You mean like Ding Dong? No, like Charleston. Where the first shots of the Civil War rang out. Fort Sumter. You know that. Everybody knows that. Without mitosis there would be nothing. What provokes change within a cell. Who's calling the shots. How the little chromosomes do their commingling and pull themselves apart. It's a miracle. So men will be men and fight each other and the women stay home and fix porridge. You date yourself, everything is equal now and no one eats porridge. You Old Goat. I always thought we'd get in a fight. Put down that slimy pick axe. I deserve to die from something much better. A bullet that never heard of mitosis. A clean bullet shot from a fishing rod. That's impossible and I'm not going to fight you. I'm going to dance in the sunset with my sister fairies. And never go fishing with the likes of you again. We're just two cells that pulled ourselves apart and can't stand each other. I'll keep manufacturing tanks and you go dance with the fairies. They don't use tanks anymore and nobody believes in fairies. So I guess we'll just live in this single cell together and never pull ourselves apart. Oh yeah? Watch this.

Not Too Late

It's too late
to procrastinate.
Fill your heart
with soap.

Cleanse
the uncleanable
and turn around
nothing.

Old
is ageless
and the new
bored.

Strike a chord
with an ancient lyre
a dodecaphonic
scale.

Every note is equal
to every other note.

Be democratic
and abstract
diddle
with dada.

Go backwards
with every
breath you take.

You are at
the steps of
creation.

Guess what?
Nobody's there.
Knock on the door.
Nobody answers.

Take your avant garde
heart back
to your own time.

Guess what?
Nobody's there.
Knock on your own door.

Is anybody home
before I get home?

Go in
and be there
for yourself.

Don't be dependent
and cry on
an unknown person's
shoulder –
who isn't there
anyway.

Attack your dreams
bring them all down
to reality.

An Offer

You're feeling isolated
that's what I feel
 can I be of any
  help to this
   a bridge
    an excuse
     to communicate
      without thought
      of any one else
      in the picture.
      An isolated thought
      meets
      an isolated thought
      over distance
      and with time
      joined.
      It's an idea
      an offer
      open
      I'm making.

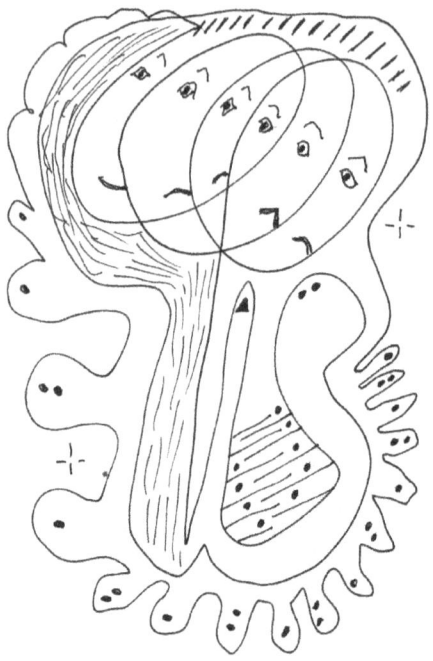

Fragile Grace

Happiness is a thrill taken seriously
and remembered pleasurably as it
disappears easily
as if nothing really can be sustained –
you remember it pulling you up
by yourself on its fragile wings
lifting, but it was a real thing
and is ongoing now that
you think about it.

Best Shared

A partner is someone you talk to
on repeated occasions
perhaps without
mutual agreement
to anything.
Someone who stays in your mind
but doesn't dominate since it's
a working relationship, a partner
in life's misgivings
in the trend toward perfection
which is a ha ha, as is
paradise
but the gift of knowing
there is this other as if
another side of you
that throws light on each other
from the succession of days
and the mutual benefit
of the heart, two hearts
thinking at once.
About the practical functions
of an emotional day
and the emotional functions
of a practical day.

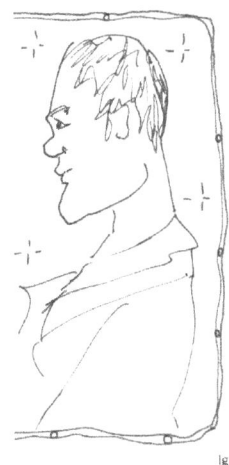

Ongoing

There is no missing the missed
    at odd times when working
concentration all –
but then relaxing from that
bolds the picture, bulls the presence
the presence of the non-presence
as the unique nature of the created
creator profoundly charmed
the one person one is when one is
    terribly one, all vibrations of a
being being *present* and doing things
    no one else is doing that when
death strikes all one *out,*
there is a sucking sound like
a vacuum of hurt, a loss –
blood drained out, memory floods in,
and no memory is adequate
    to fulfil the need of the real.

Real heart, real brain and
figure of emotional intent
the living physical no substitute
for the physical, ever.

So what is missed is all
taken away, that all gone
to the living in the present.
What do we have left,
you and I still here
with the love lost –
loss is permanent to live with
you and I, going on
ongoing, on. /10Oct2017

Machismo

Testosterone glutted machismo is killing us
almost as fast as the poison we keep pumping
into our own atmosphere.

The Bruisers

Life in the Country of God where the heinous boy friends
    stretch their wings.
They've pecked and pawed their way through women
"lifelong irritants," bullying and blustering
footballing and boxing and hockeying their way
while the good guys stay silent afraid to be called "weak."
Life in the Country of God where the heinous boyfriends strut,
they're on a permanent rut in their minds even after they're dead.
Even after their heads have been turned by a "skirt" as they call her
and they go after their prey for the last time.

Matriarchs: A Note

Matriarchs, I have known a few, some more than others. When I moved to Placitas I came to know Ann Rustebakke, Adela Amador Garcia, and Elaine Slusher who put in my hands Lou Sage Batchen's book compiled in the 30's, *Las Placitas - Historical Facts and Legends*. Adela Garcia later married Harry Wilson, minister, and they both published books from Amadore Publishers Press and Adela wrote recipe columns for *New Mexico Magazine* and of course a book, *Southwest Flavor*. Her son, Armando Garcia, was one of my best students.

Elaine Slusher's husband Arnold used to give me rides on occasion and Steve, their son, even helped me with the collating of a poetry magazine I published from Placitas, called Duende. Elaine herself, glamour model in New York and in a believe it or not transition, one of the first Anglos in Placitas, helping to bring electricity to the Village and starting the first 4th of July Parade, becoming an artist and leading art classes in the Community Center.

Matriarchs part of our lives here – Frances Escardida with kids in the school, Cristina Gonzales authoring with Vivian Delara *Conversations of the Past,* and Victoria Klemz writing, and Bernie Umland whose floor I helped tile. Foundational women among many others. And in the Little Store coming out to greet you in Spanish only, Aurelia Gurule, midwife to so many women in the Village, a gardener and a grand matriarch.

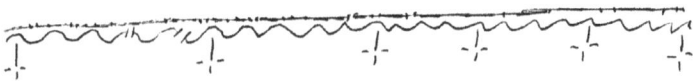

For Ann

                        Orchard of continuity
               orchard of apples pears cherry unity
          diversity, of the grapes, of the mint and flowers
      hooker's primrose, wild rose, grasses, apricots
    acequia sharer
  neighbor, story-teller, beacon of light
of what's going on - in any election
in any quarter of the Village, or history
of family, sons and daughters, marriages, births
meetings, county news, who to vote for with
good reasons, history, remember the old days the old school
the old library, who lived where, and what happened,
   food, chile, especially red chile, local produce local
      authors, everything local, comings and goings
         local products, art music, lectures, everything going on
           at the library, at the county meetings, the water board
        the disputes and the concords, who lives where and
     what happened, and all the funny stories, you know,
  we ask, we converse, you knew we asked, we
conversed. A holder of history, a matriarch, a talker,
boy what a talker. A beloved, a long standing treasure
  of our Village, the decades of change in our village.
     Longstanding, beloved, yes beloved, farmer gardener
       business woman dear to all, Ann.

love you love you love you love you love you love you love you love you love you

Common As the Rare

Fires come again and go. If you come closer to being close then that is the fire in your heart, and it sustains the burning from human need to be one with someone, someone to know you and you to know them. You have a counterpart, the season of commitment to your relationship, one that goes in and out as the day into night and day to day the week. Time insures it continues with each talk, the listening taking over and the addition to the found love with each word gets to mutual understanding, the willing availability that puts hand over heart and comes to be as common as the rare can be.

October 24

Communicate the dead
give them wings to live
as the whir of a mouthful
gives words to the air
the spirit, half vision
traces the memory
the pictures you live with
you live with every day
come alive with their voices
death does not diminish
but gives up to you
to me to us to all

a flavor of their life
that brings back reality
in full as they lived it
passes on only to us
the loved, the love
their love, our very being
made up of
what they said, what they did
adds like shadows on
the light of the living
that become part of my own
passing on, enriched in
continuity.

Tense

practice
makes
pluperfect
    .
present tense
is
au natural
    .
a verb
is
a Chinese tree
    .
nouns
abound
    .
intransitive
blocks
access

    .
gerund
rounds
out
    .
a sentence
completes
itself
    .
period
ends
where it stops
    .
future tense
is
now

/for Angus

We Sonnet

My love unfolds where it shouldn't
with absence intervening –
it whips over the distance with the desire of closeness.
What better renews than in the same room
or outside walking, say, side by side.
There's no denying it, it lives with me,
is me warmed and reminded by it.
The picture of you in my mind and
the voice calling me on the phone, through the phone.
That is the touch possible, possibly more than you think
it sustains me, this distance for now necessary.
Two different lives almost opposites
    can be the best of friends no matter what.
    It's a we thing where trust is everything.

Mountain Top

What have I been *doing* all morning?
Here I am on the mountain top of my bed
looking forward, looking backward
through the bright space of a window
featuring Autumn
indignant
indigenous
but not indigent
blessed with falling leaves
and bright sun all –
yellows and warm reds
and losing greens to brown.
Sun lights the heart
but doesn't fix
in activity
King of nothing
as it should be,
a Pauper Prince even stretches it.
I'll fist up myself to do something –
positive is as positive does –
organize this house, get rid of things
put things in place,
forever kiss opportunity.
Here it is, lover,
if I could only move up
off this bed
trying not to make love to you.

Repetition

Repetition is repeating the same thing
over & over until you realize
how different each repetition is.

Door to Door

What came to a closed door
opened another
so the way that was blocked
continued in another fashion.
The beauty drained away
but the practicality of strength
continued.
What *could* be
formed a presence
and became more vital
than what came only so far
before.
How can you compare
death and life
as they are
not at all the same
except in related genes
and such is the case
in brothers, say
and one goes away
and another comes close
not in distance
in discontinuous
and continuos talk.
Talk over, around and through
land lines, air
digital ears to mouth.
The way, disruption
and span of life.
Articulation of daily
presences –
pulls and stoppage
strivings through
daily living
grow friend, non-brother
friend, as finally

gratitude of the living

takes over
and announces to the dead
we prosper
we carry on
our new found lives.

Be good and sing a song
of love.

A Place of Skulls

The desperate reaches of the soul
we catacombed we catacombed we catacombed
after Calvary gruesome Golgatha
living by the spirit of breath we spread
and built so many churches, some weathered alone
in abandoned wheatfields.
The we lost its spirit for many of us
living among Native Americans.
The Nativity became less plausible
and fighting between factions overseas
emboldened our resolve
to return to the spirit of breath
which is the same thing – spirit, breath –
as I am grateful for everything
that has to do with the breath of every living thing.

They're Glad That You're Poor

It's not hard to find
someone who's not kind –
just meet a multi-billionaire
and find someone who's not fair.
He'd just as soon crush you
beneath his fancy shoes
and rob all of you blind
so he can be with his kind.
He sucks everything into
his domain of wealth.
He lives by deception
empowerment and stealth.
It's not hard to find
someone who's not kind.
Check out Forbes or Wall Street
the Bankers, the Petro-Pricks
or knock on our President's door.
He's glad that you're poor.

Collusion

contusion
confusion
skunk diddling flimflam
intrique
in cahoots
fraudulent double-cross congame
adventurous misadventurous deceit
connive dodge craft gyp
plot scam fast shuffle graft
practice put-up job
treacherous fram fix
in league with

cabal sedition
countermine
hookup little game complot
machination
confederacy
treason trickery
covin fix
plot to undermine and scheme
to sell an entire nation
a complete abrogation
a derelict subversion

End Times

Fierce pierce
end times colossal
devastation even
in the rubbish
as all things end
all things begin
or do they
platitudes speared
to the door
as it falls inward
and crashes down the hallway
the moving, advancing
door to nothing
finally disintegrates
in the master bedroom –
the intense smell
of feces, urine
flesh rot
and Chanel #5.

Transmission

As I refused to be
you are.
I took what I couldn't do
and made it a life
or it formed me
against everybody's wishes
in that small town
surrounded by plains –
one tiny slip of a mountain
in the distance,

but you went with the
prevailing force –
sports, combative rivalry
the normality of hunting
the toughness of the range
ranch living extremes –

I practiced music
clarinet drums piano
after tap dancing instead of
basketball –
we raised sons
and drank to oblivion
some things we have in common

and met after the death
of a mutual friend and brother.

Time brings opposites together
to figure things out.
What is shared is shared
in gratitude.

We are living to discover
all that is left
of a very fine discovery.

Mutual entertainment
of the stresses of life
thrown at us separately
individually.

That morning sun shines
leaves through the window
and the slight breeze
take me with it
outside over the distance
where we can talk
as technology steps in
ear to ear.

Noise Bank

The penitentiary of song
gross malfeasance newsing your ears
sleigh bells rung from disorder
pharmaceutical magnates
    cramming drugs down your doctors' throats
the whine of TV murders never being solved
jets crashing into cars that don't reach holiday destinations
carols of Christless Christmas penetrating the mall mobs
and store clerks punching in your latest Chinese imports

uncomfortable men and overdressed women sitting out
    the preacher and the priest
waiting to get home to loud shouting football from giant screens
    "what the hell else is TV for, mom?"
everyone bowed in any idle moment or every single moment
to each little handheld illuminated screen, the miniature Bible
    of our time
leading the way out of darkness into self-appointed delight

I don't have to attend to nobody, I don't have to listen, I hardly have
    to talk
I'm in my cell, my cell phone heaven, don't bother me
with your screeching accidents and your invectives to do something.
Give me my dope in hand or my game box at least
and what's for dinner that Sam's didn't assemble, what happened to
    the old times?
Is there any way to retreat from the madness of ads
the buy buy buy buy with your plastic non-money into further debt
there's no ring of the cash register any more, just a punch in the face
you *must* have that bloated trophy truck that everyone's buying hell
it gets 13 miles to the gallon sometimes and gas is cheap

the sounds of carols down the hall calling you to some past
what past, only cacophonous present with liars forming the nation
into a 1930's or even 19th Century or even a 3rd World banana
republic country screaming lies to adoring cults and ignorant clans

as the multi-billionaires take everything of yours
and throw it against the wall of indifference.
Compassion, what is that? What time is it? Make some noise.
I can't hear anything when it's silent.   /22Nov2017

Half Wish

Mother of God prepare me for
the Fires of Perdition or
the Angels singing dirty songs.

Tums

Tums will make you feel vibrant and young.
Tums will let you have fun
Because if you turn the pill upside down
then it becomes smut.

This Room

This room is bigger
than I deserve
perhaps I deserve only
a padded cell.
How did I acquire
such huge dimensions
so many things
so many corners to my box of life
spread out unmanageable
in every minute of every day
there's always something unseen
hidden around every corner.
I have no right to criticize the wealthy
when I'm swimming
in my own wealth.

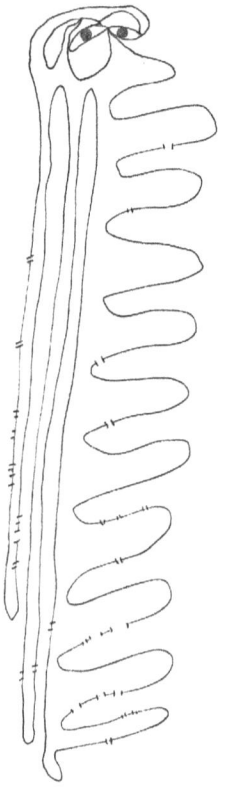

That spare cell I've dreamed about
most of my life
(my bed, my desk, a window
some books)
what a contradiction
of reality.
Thomas Merton could do it:
he's a professional.
I'm an amateur
dreamer of, as it turns out
plenitude
lost in the confusion
of my own confusion.

Getting Low

Let go of your letting, letting go of your going to let go, to rise up and let go, sit back down and let go. Let go your past present future, after you do the effort, let go of yourself to surprise.

The formulation of above, below and around may exceed your expectations, which ought to be nil. Selfish expectations will get you nowhere. So the sages say, of which I'm not one.

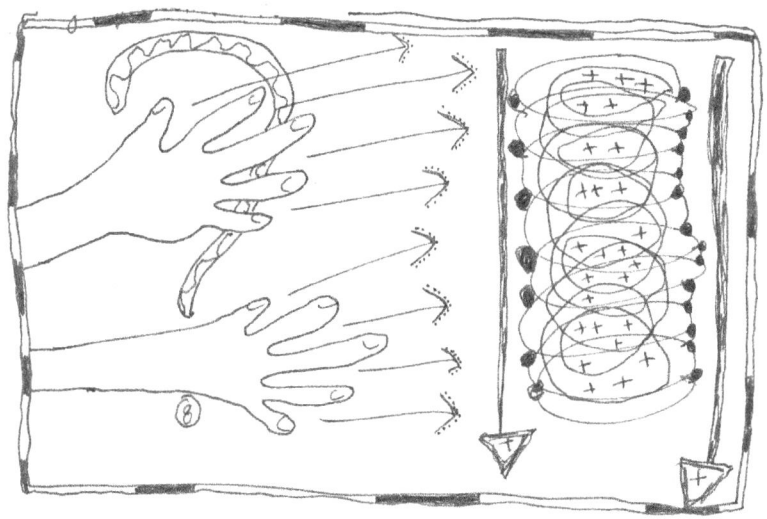

Like Me

Please like me.
Retweet me.
Like my blog.
Fill in your email address.
Join my group.
Subscribe to my channel.
Affix your fate
to my fortune.

You And I

Such
not easy
sowing
not oats
but the fine
line
of pleasure
Hearken
ancient world
that was never
ancient
to itself
we can Kiss
with thin
lips
and stimulate
the entire
universe.

Old pals
know
to embrace –
one distant
one far
stills
the imagination
with minimal
intensity
the lack
includes
the fulfilment
if seen
from both
directions
near
and far
as one ear
tells

the other
don't wait
but jump in
where all
is wet
love
takes on
airs
but needs to be
doused
once in awhile
as
it is okay
yes
yes
to love
all you
need to,
no demands
ever
being made
what is
muted
is also
the full
cathedral
organ
with a fat guy
pulling
out
stops
and a thin guy
playing
for all
he's worth
as she

and she
converse
it is not
so easy
for men
who when
opening up
takes over
they too
are sexless
as the sexed
in paradise
so help me
god
there are
two of you
"contact
with such minds
is indispensable"
sayeth
the two hands
of god
Brahma
bursting through
the symbolic door
open
thy rough beast
thy lips to
subtlety
sensitivity
empathy
the list goes
on to

eternity
amitayus
mandala
assures
long life
with Buddha
in the center
of both things
at once
and Christ
doling out
food
to the poor
igniting
faith
in everyone
the calling
to attention
in everyday
movements
we derive
our rights
from
identical
origin
all
are created
equal
in the
dispensation
of Earth
Earth planets
the yin and
the yang
as intensity
without demands
loves
to fullest
thin line

pleasure
bursts
into full
knowing
worldliness
yes
that sees
the world in
redeeming
each other
as long as
the bountiful
is on one
hand and
acceptance on
the other
as long as
there are no
rules
in the
equation
of the Earth
Father Sky
studded
with stars
of cold indifference
burning
in intensity
two things
of opposite
nature
cohabiting
or dual stars
habiting
brought down
to this warmth

the true electric
warmth of
Earth inhabitants
when reviewed
in each
other
reminded of
the generosity
of spirit
which is always
fused
in circling
one
to the other
whether male
to female
either known
or unknown
circling
each other
far
or near
digital talk
talks the human
discourse
the plant to
animal
concourse
the chat between
two things
completes
the arch
the top stone

come alive
in its compressed
vitality
sprechgesang
in all variations
of speech
of the heart
singing to
the end
of life's intent
the muted
and expansive
the free to be one's
flavorful
self
in all true
care
that good out there
needs no
door
to go through
playing
the game
of openness
Venus
and Jupiter
meet in
the early morning
sky
this morning
apparent
in the constellation
of Virgo
we meet
in innocense
to find our souls
overlap
keeping
one's distance also

floods
the heart
and soul
sole commitment
to each
other
the black
Madonna
mother to
us all
God the mother
of Ann
the Mother
of Mary
God the mother
of all
come forward in
Coatlicue
mother of
stars
stars and
stars
stars the mother
of us all
cold to hot to touch
the mother star
mother load
the loaded
word
that is
think of good
you do
rather than
just you doing
as you
tell me

what I
know
to know again
the obvious
is not so
obvious
to this idiot
human
the child
childish
in supposed
adulthood
needs
the other
cohabiter
the friend
friend to
the friend
ancient
to find
contemporary
as avant garde
art
of love
love
and the loved
hear
Lennie Tristano
Bill Evans
the piano
dances
the two hands
now four

in the mind
two voices
Fiordiligi
and Dorabella
duet
in *Cosi Fan Tutti*
Mozart
singing
he must while
playing
the piano
as the mind
already
articulated
just flows
as the water
in mountain
streams
the issuing
forth
of the divine
earth
love
in the story
of love rings
true
under the thin
disguise
of the cool
the fine line
of pleasure
vibrates
between two
people
or the creature
and person
or plant
and person
holding

the Earth as
habitable
as
the powers that be
pull back
forced by
survival
to see
what I see
in the gentle
touch,
the hard slap
of reality
what is clear
oh husbandman
survivor of the
universe
now gardener
hunter
caretaker
blessed woman
spirit
the feminine
returned to
her rightful
station
after being
deposed since
before the Old
Testament
that old
lie about
male dominance
now crackles
and burns
in the stove

of the past
we are now
in the dharma
of the new
way
ever open
to surprise
ever empathetic
and allowing
the humble
to be
strong
as is
its natural
want
we
you and
I
yes, we
you
and I.

/13Nov2017

Closest One

Come alive and survive
as the shells of death
are left behind –
a new, a renewed
 clean heart opens
  to love.
   Congratulations
    a true survivor
    a prospector
     of natural wealth,
      a grip of a disease
       releases to the family
        of love and healing.
         Anybody has particular
         failings, the ravages
        of hard living, but
       the glow of building strength
      builds through it all
     and family, small or large,
    can sing the seasons,
   the ups and downs, and prosper,
  be a true flavor
 of the good life
and bind to
remarkable balance
and endurance,
beauty, appreciation
faith in the renewing
Earth and the health
of our love.

Mantra of Care

Powers of the mind, powers of the body
there is no poetry here
the mantra of care
care Blue Buddha, Healing Buddha
budding out
perfect lotus ascends between us
strong-arms poetry into action
get to work, the perfect face between us
    Christ, St. Francis, Mary, Anne
the Cathedral resonating in the Hogan
desert plane of sunset arroyo canyon
echo walls, the low pedal organ
the wind making no sound, the stars out
    to blink all night
ah as you hear it, resonating breath
mantra of care
ah as you hear, the music of healing unheard
resonating in the bones hearing itself, resonating
blood and nerves, all points of body connected –
the harmony reaches from the mind out and the body up.

The music interior as parts interrelated play –
you lie down in the body mastery
the interweaving like a blanket of the soul,
the kind and bouncing spirits as the drum dances
the heart beating flowing through all, the mending,
the character of your clear design allowing
the Good Orderly Direction to stand up within
the direction of healing order, blessings as these songs sing
directions North in, South in, West in, East in,
Above in, Below in flowing, the sound you lie within
letting go into the hand of Nature, the moving hands
the rest, the mystery, the minute world harmonies –
love blesses where you are, all through you and
the spheres in which you live as you mend, renew,
become true self again, as we all are, at our best in
the mantra of care.

                                               for Joel Dec2017

Good Morning

Envelop, include, enthuse
from dawn wanderings in cold air
come in, come on in from outside.
Enveloping, including, enthusiastically
warm up inside from coming in outside
cold clear morning with the windswept canyons
where you have been.
Come in, warm up, include.

———————————————

Be a vigorous displeased spirit
as you are
are is am ————————

Be a virgin in disguise
be a reprobate
a dirty old man virgin!

Nonsense that drives the world
speak to me of faith
faith that moves mountains.
Can't you see where they were?
There's nothing there that previously were
the Sandias.
Whoops! I meant
the Alps.

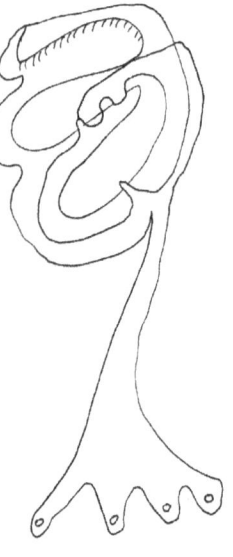

———————————————

Prayer –
a hop skip and a jump to the source
the source, of course
is made up of many many sources
so which are you hopping to
perhaps the source of yourself –
pick a star.

Fizznew

The bottom of my cave
is covered with cellphones.
They crackle when I walk.
- *Fizznew*

Gravitational waves
wave back at me
when I ride my mind's
rollercoaster.
-*Fizznew*

The simple life
is all you need -
the sun rising up
to poke you in the face.
-*Fizznew*

Bye Bye Net Neutrality

Freedom is not good enough
take it away
give to the major channels
control of your minor channels.
Small business is irrelevant
take it away.
Fast speed?
Take it away unless you pay –
pay, pay, pay
so says the Republican head
of US Federal Communications
Ajit Pai, Pai says
pay pay pay.
Forget freedom
that's for another day.
Net neutrality is extinct
like the dodo bird
gone away.
So says Ajit Pai
another tool of the corporate world –
if you're small go away
but whoever you are
pay pay
or you become another drip
from a frozen jar of molasses
one drip per day
of internet non-speed
unless you pay, Pai says
you're insignificant
unless you pay pay pay.

Masculine Spirit

   Don't let your male guard down
  that slight swagger when you walk
 covers the clinched fist.
What could have been hand to hand
father to son
backed off and you got a spanking,
 a hand that hurt over and over.
 And when you began to reach out
  in your physical mind
  there was no one there.
  The mother of all love
  came to your rescue
  in sympathy
   but it wasn't enough
    of what your ache wanted.
    Where was the masculine of brother
    the friend of understanding?
    Tough love without the love
     took over.
     The bruise of hitting in sports
      the acting jaunty, the spitting,
     the talking down others
      that weren't up to standard,
      the facade blending in your nature
      whether you liked it or not,
       put-downs and competition
     the way of conversation.
     Bringing you up into who you are
    who are you, now,
   built on that lack
that continues.

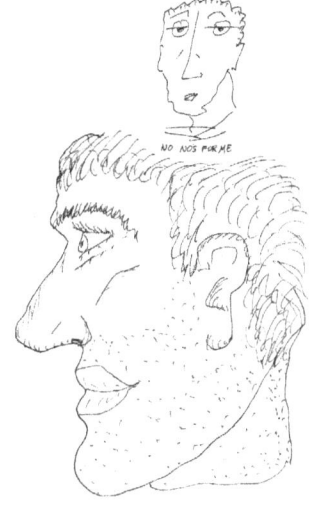

Belief

You can only believe what you do not know
you can only retrieve one frog at a time.
Being caught up in nonsense
we sang the history of the divine.

- - - - - - - - - -

Are you a realist or an abstract bouffant?
Do you prefer dreidels to ordinary spin toys?
If your face is removed can you face off?
Did hell open up and kiss your heaven?
Has everything been exorcised?

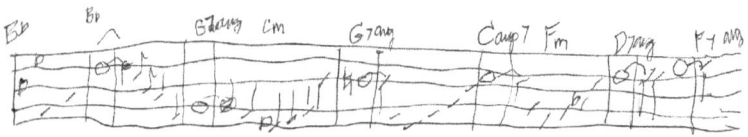

The Song In You

Did you sing songs falling out time?
Was the registration correct?
Whose name was the impetus?
Did it soar out of the cathedral
and become autumn leaves?
Did time come once, twice
and become one with the chorus
or was it all just you humming
in your voice in your mind
as the tune played over and over.
Who gave you permission to make up song?
was it freedom of voice
or the composer in you went to sleep
and you heard the oldest tune imaginable?

Dawn Song

Thank you's are in order, Thank You said.
Gratitude filled the moment,
a far-reaching dimension took over.
The appreciation reached out and out
encompassing Jupiter
    in the very early morning Southern sky.
Dawn was apparent any moment.
Could I keep this mood all day
    this warmth of alertness
    the profound in the minuscule to the magic?
You didn't see that, did you
all those colors come out of nothing
from the magician's hand, the science of logic
expanding out in ever new ways. /24Dec

The Light Bounces Through

Satisfaction with sight improves to the point of natural Kodachrome
where everything in the protected set around you vibrates.
For those seeing, this is infancy.
Full adulthood is a barrage of the senses, difficult to keep up
    with the orchestra of daily living.
Awe soon dissipates into ordinary boredom, or worse, depression
where the world closes in to nothing. What good is the miracle
    of seeing
the long trek of evolution to get to this gift, and hearing
and all the others? I'd rather have my self *dispute* everything,
put blinders on, submit to the halter of one ordinary direction
full of myself to the point of a pulling stagnation, irritation.
Burst free! Reminders boil over on the stove.
    "Watch what you're doing,"
I tell myself. "Open up, throw off, wiggle and shake off!"
The light bounces through the window and greets me walking out
    the hallway. /24Dec2017

Morning /25Dec2017

What is birth, is it a first, can it renew -
whose birth, a prophet's? A far away figure?
Can it be a season, a beginning of a year
a transplanted birth to make it work?
Is it an everyday birth, a beginner's world every second?
A constant ongoing renewing of now.

Is the baby the baby of eternal babyhood? Bye-bye,
I can't sustain an archetype of eternity.
But give me the new of every living thing
right at the beginning if everything else is swept away.
A fresh start splashes me in the face in the morning
which, I'm told, is an old practice before greeting the sun,
the sun I am in the morning as I greet it, *lucky me*
to be born in a cycle and be reborn again, and again and again.

Water Creek Swallowtails Rocks
Las Huertas Canyon
(after a photograph by Lenore Goodell)

Does the sky, gray, titillate
send you into pleasures of rain
or, crystalized, snow.
What is snow, white and the seven
rain buckets filled –
temperature hinges unhinges
the water particles
the macro in consort with
the micro
the mysterious relations
science finds little about more and more
as we advance, wishing to be wonder-eyed
at the large picture.

The small picture - pixels swallowtails -
rushing creek water
the advance of seasons
the mountain and sky contributing all
we wait on.
See the possibility? Refreshed pine forest?
Water to drink? Gardens?
We are everyplace in time, aren't we?
At least I am, even
on my knees.

Loving Someone

Stop feeling guilty
about loving someone –
you make no demands
but let it flow out
from your warm heart.
It's a gift to be in the light
of this transforming
into high voltage
the zapping satisfaction
your electricity stimulates –
you are a good companion
near or far
a good ear
a solid support
if need be –
there when called
here always here
where love starts
and continues

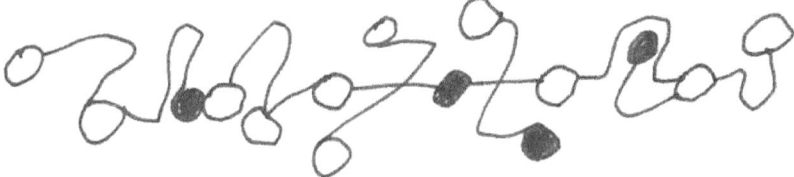

Our Father who's smart in Heaven
    is dumb on Earth where
Mother takes over.

THUNDER
Poems - 2018

Water Chant

Rain royal roost romance register report
rest roast rue refer regal roam rain tone
tune ton talk toe ray ream rural rococo
wind winding wonder one under roost
tuck wow woman rain rack till tow the most
muck water mock tone real is it real rain.

Mono Color

It's as if the plants have all taken on one color
the color of dehydration.
Desiccation has set in on our morning walk
    in the wide arroyo.
If brown is desiccation it's supplanting the green.
The persistent green junipers are dusty and pale.
Sparse juniper berries attracting no birds.
The brownish loss of life from the wintry drought
seems more urgent as dehydration comes comes with
the unseasonable warmth.
Climate change stalks the Earth with its manmade curse
    of death
as the megalomaniacs in their high chairs fight change
and lead humankind towards cyclical extremes
    of morbid weather.

Sing snow in spite of all, sing water, sing collapse of
    the oligarchs of oil
bankers and realtors of stagnation and self-absorbed idiocy.
Sing snow, sing water, to ring from the impossible some healing
as massive numbers of people take on their own strength
forcing change to Earth, self sufficiency and renewables prosper
as the voting booth is the turning point of the Earth
as it turns out as we turn out in defense of our Mother planet.

Sing snow in spite of all, sing water, sing sanity and science
sing for the return of natural order, shared wealth, compassion
for plants as well as animals, *sing snow,* sing water sing for
    the sanity of truth, as I walk back to the car and return,
the dryness and crazy warmth hounding me. /1Jan2018

Here and Now

Some day there will be a reckoning
and that reckoning will hit you over the head with positives
not aligned with any faith or doormat
but the door itself, a key and opening to
the goal you've been looking for that vibrates warm
through your body.
                uuuuuuuh!   *(oo as in "tool")*
a mission, a tad hopeful, so *that's* what I'm all put together for.
A harmony where we interconnect and do, the cells of my body
and my self, we are working together and this bigger thing
    so big outside of me
is pulling me to do bit by bit what I do, what do I do?
All my organization of my self and functions is ready to do it
    now. /5Jan2018

They Threw Me Out

They threw me out of the artificial asshole
    they erected for that purpose.
"Why do you veer off into music, drawing,
    and painted sticks?
Your lack of sustained focus on poetry is abominable.
You have no position at a University
you must be removed from our sustained self-focus.
The Jewels of Poetry must remain uncontaminated by your ilk
your lightness, your own garbage intellect.
So we have erected a giant publisher's asshole and, for the last time,
    we are ready to expulse you.
What do you have to say?"
They threw me out from where I'd never been in the first place.

Scattering Voice

From all particles of the East
wetting particles of the North
dampening those in the West
drenching those in the South
rain vesicles, rain channels
rain droplets hitting the dust
the smell arising and dampening
the nostrils.

Powers that fabricate the overall design
we call on you, I call upon your grace
we who've committed errors
some slight, some abominable.
We patronize your powers
and urge an end to drought.
A drought in winter freezes pipes
and threatens no water
the absence of real snow
on our near mountain
promises nothing in the summer
but waiting for the scarce   rain.

As the wait gets longer and longer
as we've poisoned the planet
and the atmosphere,
beginning to heat ourselves
almost to extinction
you can come and bring us health
to reconnoiter, reassess, reconstitute ourselves
to recognize your eternal
maternity
powers that bite through the dust
bringing water to satisfaction
filling the barrels and the pipes
entering the dirt to meet the seeds,
gushing down arroyos
readying for
the February thaw and the spring to life to come.

Rain only is the master, master water
your saving grace a source of life
from all directions of the East
wetting directions of the North
commingling and wetting directions of the West
fulfilling gushing falling from the South
the clatter of rainwater, flowing
coming down all around
turning the famished upside down
as the spirit of the call calls
opens up so the voices can be heard
out there, up there, around there
from a voice down there we
encourage it up to you
powers of the hanging on above
striking through the clouds building
building and building in harmony
to the thunder, the echo, the lightning
accompanying the fulfilling fall
of rain dancing as it falls
to our need the turning to snow
as it freezes covering growing
snow pack of winter
rain and streams come later
come now
to the grateful water watering the need.

Gratitude is now, raining snowing
filling the sky with damp drench
overflowing from all directions
the thirst wetted, wettened, lasting
growth to come, green into flowering
flowering from the flowing to come.

Gravitational Waves Are Only the Beginning

Mother of phenomenal carriage, ever present and yet still.
Featureless and beautiful. Silent and yet made up of language.
The language of body mind, of words unheard.
A presence that is unmistakenly absent and yet
falling together inside you from a beacon far distant.
A museum of the heart next door to the museum of the soul.
Walking through half naked are you looking at, absorbing
or being looked at, absorbed, what is that click of light?
Or is it a transmission of words you usually don't say, you never say
an expression, a denotation in a sculpture before you?
Or are you moving having stepped off your pedestal
and expanded into Americana, pop presence, connection of voice,
disparate unions, cerebral cortex meets the moon and stars
    and gravitational waves
so infinitesimal you may have lost it or can't keep up with it.
Or a barren spot just takes over or everything is done
and she didn't say anything, or you said nothing. and just listened.

Accident Pleasure Or Informed Insouciance

Avoid the secondary.
Follow through the first odd
juxtaposition of words

(In writing)

Handshake

He's got me in the palm of his hand.
He's taken his hand away
and left me here to stay.
Thus is the monoculture
of man to man.

Be The Light Within

"Be the light within.
It is yours.
Carry on without the snag
of controlling others.
Selfishly positive is alright
so you can be useful.
Who knows who might carry on
what's within you.
Knowingly, unknowingly
someone's world turns."

One to Another

One voice to another
another one makes two
to bend an ear
to hear one better
takes opening half of the mind
at least.
What did you say about
the love in your life
the waning problems? No

waxing only
to get worse –
what is better
than expressing them
out
out of the darkness
the light of hearing –
life bowls both of us over
every once in awhile
maybe daily.

It's Better to Love Than to Not

Can you fall in love when you're ancient?
You're darn tootin!
It pulls and tugs the rug out from under you.
Nothing you can do about it.
Delish.

On The Physical

All love, the most passionate love
is a mind-set
a mind-set set up by your hormones.
Hormones sing your destiny.
True, you're attracted to a real body
and crave physical when you can't have it
but in your mind the fantasy advances the play-out
directed by your hormones.
I create a cinema of longing
based on the person
which takes over the content of the mind
completely separate from the *real* person –
hormonal disharmony of reality.

Hormonal Blast

Over and over I ask to the darkness
from whence the configuration that channels my love
that determines how I look at things
am attracted to or repelled or just indifferent.
Is it hormonal DNA, or hormones that bend everything
    to their given whim.
I look out and see, according to them, a whole lifetime
balanced on their need, if it is a need. Their way
becomes my way as a turning towards someone
just that one, or those few, very few compared to
the mass of humanity, suddenly there's a lock on,
an obsession, a pleasing connection that draws toward
relentlessly and then it becomes a frustration that seems
    almost endless,
as the day blends into the night of your hormonal need.

The Learning Curve of Death

The learning curve of death and dying is starting,
in speaking about writing he chortles endlessly
"Why do you wrap yourself up in cake?
Is it Viennese or common old ordinary chocolate?
Stop eating black bottomed pie, remember it's white on top."
The dogs are barking under the blue moon.
At a certain time you can celebrate diversity
    and then forget about it the rest of your life.
Chocolate is parting, strawberry is a kiss
    angel food is completely without worth.
If everything starts in the kitchen where does it end up?
Did you have a lot to say before you shut up
    and tried to smile with your lips closed?
What does your heart want. Did you get up
    and drink a glass of water?"

What Was Our Face

Does the encounter of police on Avenue B have anything to do
    with the encounter of Jesus on Avenue A.
And the disturbed women of history on Avenue C?
And the artists all camped out on Avenue D?
Do you destroy everything that held up humans from varmints
    by going backwards?
What is the reason for your goose-step backwards into the anus
    of back history?
Back back why do you say back, oh reality master?
The idiots with power are saying it's forward as
we all know, they are dragging the World Earth backwards
against its will, from the only direction of sanity.
What's going on on Avenue E and in the countryside of hope?
Is your bomb getting ready to explode in your face, our face.

Particles of Wisdom

Don't hurry anything up. Be your own apprentice.
Emmet Fox says don't think of the difficulty, think of God.
But what is God?
God is the make up of particles of wisdom within.

Dark Interior

My friend is the dark interior of the mind
where the real thoughts lie,
the uncovered up covered up.
But I can see beneath the blind
since I live with the thirst for truth.
And privacy is not everywhere but here.
Do you see it? What is your fear?
That your favorite little place will be exposed?
What is it, really, the kiss of reality?

Pop Music

Even the women have falsetto voices
and the men have gone beyond that
    to monotone staccato talk
or the gutter of damaged vocal chords
yortling screams come from the opposite ends
    of each while
electronic hand claps 2nd and 4th beat
relentlessly applaud themselves.

Flavor of Innocense

The flavor of innocense, is it an unknown is it an unknown
    is it a bone to pick?
Is it so many Charlestons dancing on the head of a pin?
A pin turned into a sword to a lord in hysteria over
    the people he picked to put on this planet
behind her back when she wasn't sure she wanted any,
any people at all who always lost their sense of innocense
and indulged in the debacle of craving, the madness of overrunning
    limitation.
So she could say "I told you so," but you had to toy with it,
    you always have to toy with it.
Look at what you've got, what we've got, a plagued earth.

He grumbled and left the spaceship and went off to
    console himself in the mysteries of what was left of Nature.
Perhaps out there somewhere will be my cosmic twin, male
    or female or intersex
and we can dance again like we did in youth.
But always she was there reminding him of his previous self
    before he turned human.

Ah

A star for your mind,
a moon for your thoughts –
a galaxy for your inspiration.

Ms Nature

"I'm going in there
and prepare the flowers for blooming.
I do all this for free,
collapse the universe on my knee
and spring up as all springs up
and we're here again – you & me."

Conversations

In secret I taste your conversation
a bit one sided but full of the world you know.
It all started when I spoke of someone dear to both of us
and you grabbed me when I walked over
and something passed through time.
A major loss said okay to both of us
or it has to be at some point, ok.
After someone dies after awhile you have to
pick up where you left off.
Although everything is altered
the procedure is different as if you're
working around something –
that gap between is a conversation that
draws us together even over long distances.

In Love

How can you say you're out of love when
you're in your own heart?
And you can love all you want out
to anyone you're drawn to.
So you are full of love even when not
returned to. That person must pick up on warmth
from you, anyway. You are a more complete human being
for loving, intensely as you do.
The compassion increases, you are electric
in hearing what the other says
and a confident in the truest sense.
Let this boundlessness be, and with no demands
thankful you are led to someone in such high regard
whose life you can help articulate.   /16Mar2018

Hallelujah

It doesn't matter save a dollar go to France
get out of here, discover Romance.
    Oh la la dance dance dance!
Give it all up for pleasure, the zeal of discovery
envelope yourself in new vistas.
All those travel agencies need you to call
and you know you can do it, go to a safe land
a land of knickerbockers or Swiss cheese
or astounding monumental sculpture and
    bumpy camel rides
a place that's black and white and you meet Tarzan and Jane
a place where bananas and pineapple and palm trees
    fill the scenery
a place of extraordinary chasms and donkey rides to oblivion.
Get up and go where there are monasteries and incense
    and caves to meditate in.
You're all ready, book everything, get up and go
    leave your feisty troubles and shout hallelujah!
And just be sure to leave your mind behind.

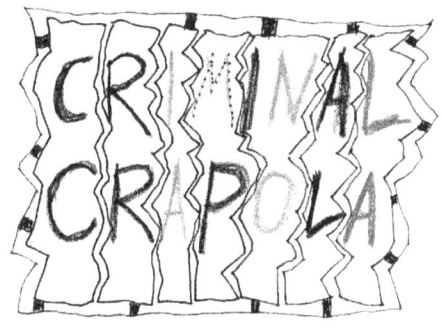

Criminal
crapola
Crimini!
Crime takes over
in the billionaire botches
of Washington.
The coach of cash
the rubber lips of lies
the laundered silos of
dirty moolah
towers of empty condominiums
monuments to the apotheosis
of greed —

the gag of Republican dishonor
& spineless ass kissing
as their majority rule rules to
suppress opposition.
Where does it fall,
from the tall treachery & treason
into the healthy hands of resistance?
It can only fall from the bloated
weight of its own failing
backstabbing its way to deflation
& total collapse,
power hungry ego
a spoof of lying nonsense
idiots
blubbering their way into the past.

Musing About It

After spending most of my life thinking the Muse
     was feminine
I wondered what if he was a man.
Not all men are beasts worthy of being deported.
A masculine figure could be pointing the direction
actually giving directions –
dictation, but not a dictator.
After all, any man comes from a woman
so what's the difference?
The feminine sphere of warmth and gestation
is always there to be believed –
the humming in the dark, the accurate word song
the revelation in a creative turn of the obvious
presented in a new way. "What's to think" you say,
"A curious way of saying things," I do say.

Deception

Time strolled by
and we believed it
until we discovered
it was ahead of us –
way way ahead of us.

Brothers and Sisters - Or What

What is it like to be a brother? Is it like a friend, evidently not since I know brothers who aren't friendly or whose mutual existence seems unimportant. But what is it like to know you come from the same womb. Doesn't that demand you be close lifelong? Or having a sister, the same thing?

Students

The students are better than the teacher
as the old dries up into
beautiful incrustations.

Talk It Out

He was bound to be different. Not like the others who are all like themselves. He brought himself forward and talked about himself but not just himself, those around him. But only to me when he was talking did I hear him. And this encouraged me to listen as if favoritism was all mine and I was lifted up by it, by all the others disappearing since they weren't near and would generally not bother to open any communication with me. But he did. So the shell was broken. It was like a birth inward.

Have you ever wanted to talk to someone but couldn't or you didn't or they weren't anywhere near. Were never near. Or maybe you didn't know them. Or more likely you knew them well, very well, but they were a long way away or maybe even dead. Or they were not that far away but for some reason there was no talking back and forth, no calling, no coming by, no going there, just nothing, knowing you are friends but with little or no concourse.

So the isolation that shouldn't be set in. Was it circumstance, lack of action. Was it aging. Was it self-imposed? Was it just the flow of time gone by leaving things farther apart. Laziness? Fear drawing oneself in. A retiring? A weakness. Even a sickness. Or none of this. Just the way things turned out to be.

And this happened. A jolt in the atmosphere. A mutual loss that was an introduction, a hearing back and forth of two people who knew of each other but that was all. And then when we talked about our mutual loss we began to gain each other. As simple as that. A pouring out, a listening in. A building of acceptance from the beginning trust. Trust opened the heart in each of us. A talking it out, an acceptance that human beings need each other.   /18Mar2018

For Lenore

As we've lived so long so long to the past
and hello to now – now is the time to celebrate.
You can celebrate by just being together
for after all isn't that the new season every day?
As best I can, as best you can? Your time turns upward
and ever outward to the plants just emerging
with you on this day those little rosettes of
evening primroses, for instance, up by the creek.
It is astonishing how nature preserves hope.
What is to find, what is to find in the outdoors
which is the real truth of diversity.
We are just visitors in a world that brought us together
almost like one season turning into another.
Love is the basis for everything that clicks
for everything that is worth hearing, for everything
that renews, as we do, as the day opens up again.
       Happy Birthday 20Mar2018

Immensity

> Hubble –
> he unhitched the universe
> set everything
> free

Listening to Arnold Schoenberg's Piano Music

Take us to Tuesday while leaving us there go do the groceries.
Do 'em good or we won't be there when you get back.
You're an entity of verbal wit so why don't you say something.
You are eleemosynary. Without me you'd have
no vacuum, have no fluff, or rubber diapers.
Your groceries are tied to heaven. Yes, heaven
exists on your bathroom floor. Are you back
or did you slide and fall down, scattering everything
you bought. You're poverty-stricken. They threw you
out of the store. Pick me up. I'm delicate. It's all
a sham. You have absorbed me and stolen all
my money. It's hesitation any way. What's for supper?
You want me to make or break you? Why did you get green olives
when I told you to get black?
Let's replace everything with what wasn't there before.
Blue waves. Red Sails. Brown ships. Egg on your brow.
You've come home! We're all okay or we wouldn't be here.
Love is a baby. We haven't any. Oh wait. That's what we are.
Back to the womb! We can't make it out there. We will ourselves
fast until we can afford a cat. Oh I forgot, we own the world
and the world owes us everything. Isn't it darling
to be sitting pretty? But how can we eat when
all the food is on strike?

Diversity

No one clocks diversity: it runs fast, it runs slow
but it's always in the know: it's smarter than the blocks of one
that run themselves down – down all the way to the ground
    and below.

The Dawning – 2018

Is there peace on the other side of the mountain?
Is there peace on the other side of the river
Is there peace on the other side of the world, somewhere?
Is there a place where men and their toys don't
    go after one another?
Is there any peace in the hearts of the oligarchs
    or is it all greed and spite and control?
Is there a relaxation of hatred anywhere?
A lessening of the build up of weapons
a realization of the softening of the heart.
Or are we stuck in this down course ever down down
into mistrust and vanquishing of the poor?
Must the powerful break every rule on Earth
    that stands for health and heart and humanity?
Must religions war with each other
    and men rule every nation and enterprise on Earth?
Some breakthrough has occurred as we celebrate the youth.
Some nations have allowed their women to speak freely
    and take over the sick yearning of male dominance.
And the young who've had enough of violence and greed
    are standing up for a renewed consciousness
hearing "my religion is kindness"
and resurrecting to this day the powerful notion of compassion,
cooperation and creativity in everything they do.

Is there democracy on the other side of the mountain
    or the world somewhere
or in our own back yard?
Democracy that again will save us from tyrants
    and break down the "morbidly wealthy"
that are sucking every bit of worth out of life?
Deep down within, everyone appreciates the dawn
    which is coming, out the window, now.
And it is young and it is powerful and it is light.

                                          /Easter morning

Journal Page

You can't capsize eternity
no matter how brusque your approach towards morality.
You'll have to stand naked before the public.
+
It doesn't matter does it
it's all a flim-flam
the toast is burnt
you weren't hungry anyway
for truth.
All you wanted was to
stamp your name on
the belly of Earth
to own as much of it
as you could, and would
and can.
What will stop you
but your own indecency
your cruelty to those
who love you and
mistakenly think
you're a human being.
But maybe that's the problem –
you're all there is
and the rest of us are nothing
no power

no say so
we are not the new
human being
you have evolved
into that.

Who are we anyway
but stumbling blocks
to be kicked out of the way
as you advance.
+
Don't hit me.
Evolve backwards into substance
where love weaves the whole
thing.
+
I cried on Athena's shoulders.
She was wresting me from
yet another problem
in space.

Mother Nature

(put on bloodshot Halloween eyes)

Litter away
buy your cases of plastic bottles
suck your sugar concoction through plastic thrown away straws
add fire to the fuel of what it's like to be human
Bud-Lite your camping trails
plastic lid and plastic bottle your life of paradise
the ocean mountains of waste follow you
wherever you go in your trophy trucks and palatial
    stick frame houses
your bloated too big for your britches disposal-of-everything
madness, washed down every stream and toxic river
to this horrifying earth-hate of human population glut
throwing everything away rich and poor a cancerous species
no better than any gluttonous insect in mounting hordes
destroying its host with self incriminating delight.

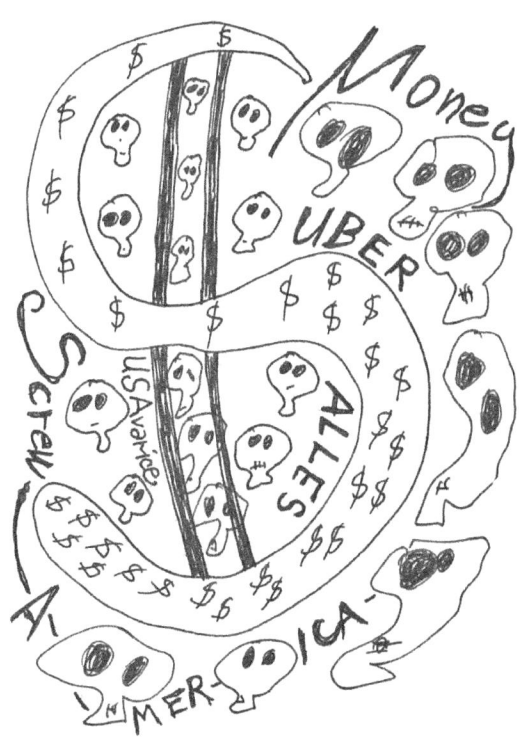

He

He filled every vacancy with filth.
He was the top dollar of the bottom feeder.
He twisted every office into a nightmare of incompetency.
He dumb-dumbed the dumb
and squeezed sense until it became senseless.
When he was done he walked away wealthy
from the ruins of an entire country.

Loner Freedom

Such freedom of the alone, take –
or have I become unplugged from the universe?
Or has the universe become unplugged
from one of its favorite planets?
And thus I'm seriously awry,
like dangling free
too far from the heart
it's not just me.
There's something disconnected
from the center of all.
All awe is disappointed
"these going alone-ers
where do they think they're going
going going going where?"

Oh such freedom disconnected from everything else
everyone else.
Filling the vacuum with a hole.
Time marches on.
The skies collapse.
When are we going to bring ourselves back
from unanticipated loneliness?
Take a giant hypodermic needle
and inject us with cooperative bacteria
or something that has some sense.

Love in Quotes

Nothing comes to me
in this spare moment
when love should
which is always a cover up
for the real thing.
The real thing is
a hormonal twist
you're the subject of
thinking it is love
to reach out and long for
to have your feelings pulled out
away from you
extending into space
towards the one
you love.

What Is Love

And yet the feeling
overpowers
riding the sensitivity
out
over borders of states
if that is the posit.
And would extend halfway
around the world
if that dreaming
fantasy of reality
directs it.
Love doesn't have to be near
to be powerful.
Just watch out –
what is it?

A Patchwork of Enigma

Remember the rolling dark that remembered everything
in spots and patches that was so intense
in moving along then in the light of the present?
It must be submerged, says the mind as meaningless time
sweeps along clearing space for more light to dark.
But those persistent patches that spot the mind
are as clear as day today just a parade of vignettes
that march through 50 years or how many
adding authenticity to life, life knowing what it knows
in its spotted career. Could I expand each out
there would be a story to tell, the weaving of
the creative mind, but there seems no connecting of the pearls
no beating back the darkness that will move over all –
but I write the spots and flashes down as anyone should.

Good Hands

Old friend, you just woke a dead ghost
an attraction toward 2 of the most beautiful hands
on a man. As the silence of years broke open
a phone call, a voice of pure presence
trying now to jump back many years
when it was full face throttle.
Two separate worlds that
know each other again.

Gun Down

Pull your weapons out of nowhere and dissolve them somewhere.
But you won't. Your extension of testicular agony is all you have
    for painful fun and young man adoration.
As the salty old men chew on cigar stubs and tap the stars on
    their collars or pull their American flag tie
        even tighter
their brilliant white skin glistens like
    the back end of a pizza
and the blood in their eyes pulses with the hip pumps
    they're giving to that porno star or common ordinary whore.
They fund to the sky engineered weapons of deceit and send
    mercenary serfs out in danger zones unprotected
launching missiles provoking dumb presidents, idiot fool dictators
to accelerate, provoke, attack bloat-face into war, tomfoolery of
    a species toughening from the growing numbers demanding
        more space.
Destroy for peace, propagandize to keep on keep on going Big
Business, on the table, under the table, throw in the table Corporate
    Warfare ain't easy but fun to turn all business over to
the weapons, technology terrifies drone dream disasters,
    weaponizing the entire
face of the species, don't look in the mirror you'll see your ass
    covering every
inch of Earth as you blot out the sun, and you sit down smiling
    to take your colossal military dump.

Going Forward

As the pianos reach up to the moon
there is only one thing to say that is
under the real behind the real around it.
As you stretch the real you will maintain sobriety
of thought and all the particles of any object
explode into view and the massive universe it's
connected to jolts you with reason and the
great big portrait of science. It's something you can eat.
Take it with you in your backpack or in the trunk of your car
as you travel fast without a foot on the accelerator.

Deflation

Forgive me for not being
who you thought I was –
a creative
exemplar
when I'm more of a
skinny
Elmer Fudd.

Poetica Pills

Poets demand prescriptions for Lyrica these days, number one in demand from the poetry doctor. But a few do ask for Sonneta. Very few demand Epica although still available. Some poets demand prescriptions for Concreta and always, of course, Limericka. But most commonly demanded of their poetry doctors is Freeversa or Progressiva. What most doctors actually prescribe, however, without telling their patients, is *(whisper)* Monologa, a common generic, which seems to work with most poets without their ever knowing it. Most are under the impression they're taking Academica or Slama or Rappa for their afflictions. Little do our poets know what they're really swallowing. *Monologa.*

Nature's Miracle Pill

Ask your doctor for *Placebo*, Nature's closest friend. It strengthens the mind and cures with elementary strength! *Placebo* is mild and natural - agrees with everybody's system - promotes the healing of body mind & spirit - the only pill with NO side effects. Demand Nature's miracle pill Placebo!

What Is the Screw
That Screwed Everything

What is the screw that screwed everything
that unscrewed itself then screwed itself down tight to bursting
and then kept screwing until all its threads
tore everything apart? The screw that screwed
beyond screwed to the hopelessly screwed condition
we're all in now?

Democracy

Bring life to life again
dying from a would-be tyrant and his
physical admixture of destructive toxins
and bloated self-image
the cracks and fissures growing
as everybody sane watches on stunned
and the powers of compassion
common sense and civility
enter the vain image
to infiltrate it . . .

sounds like a good idea
life in life again!
as the dead plasma floats away
in the desiccating swamp
of Mussolini, Hitler,
Cheney, Putin, Stalin
Kim Jong-un fellow
enemies of the people because
their only enemy
is Democracy. /23Jun2018

Heterosapien

How much rest do you need before you come back
    like a power ghost flailing at the wind?
Do all pajamas carry poisons that infect you when you sleep?
Is your tea laced with strychnine? Your bowling ball smeared with
    an obnoxious flesh-eating substance?

Are you afflicted with ennui that turns you into soup?
Have you lost your pleasure in doing anything at all
    because tarantulas and centipedes wait in your extra shoes?
Has your mother disowned you and your father sent you to Florida?
Have you drowned in the flood from Hurricane Vixen?
Have your lips been sealed and your will blinded?
In other words, have you lost your personality
    and dumbed yourself down to below the bottom?

Wake up! It's not too late, you're the soul of humanity.
You still have a brain and if you close your eyes and stop farting
    so much you still have some common sense.
You might still add a brain cell to the 2 you have left if you listen to
    your Coach Mother Nature and stop tackling fierce idiots
and damaging your brain at the bottom of every dog pile.

Come on out from under and face up to the mirror image of your
environment, the you that's disappearing in the center of yourself,
the tiny you among the giant flowers and magnificent wild animals
and all creatures that have inherited the Earth instead of
    spitting on it.

Silence

Nothing comes to me and the silence is provocative –
the breeze gentles my skin from the window
the curtain in motion –
Mozart takes up harp and flute in the old familiar tune –
nothing is familiar, when you get older, but memories.
Where does the dawn lie in this picture several hours off.

Did You Say Garden?

Do you talk tomatoes do you talk bell peppers
do you talk broccoli all the vegetables we don't have now
from the garden that was but never is now, the water a vacancy
in a high-rent district, the skies as dry as the earth that blows away
and leaves you with the grit in your mouth and heat bearing down
but gritting forward with the high sophistication of the mind
balanced on a substanceless conversation and a rain barrel down
to scummy water at the bottom. No talk of jalapeños let alone
cabbage or lettuce and spinach. Long gone with the water
drained away, evaporated like the mind gone after it, crazy
world gone hot drifting off in space coughing do you hear
the coughing of everything on the red dust the black dust the color
of every color but the rainbow, the lost mist, the muss of the mind
the endless talking of nothing to talk about – did you say garden?

One More Year (on my 83rd)

One more year and the fits complain
the fights break out the protests mount
suffering is intended from the top down
the leakers go to town and spill all
it is revealed it is revealed the Bible
is opened to the oppressed word as manicured fingers
search to find supportive words
Christ who would never be a Christian is left out
as, again, the evil force of dominance & pressure
is put on everybody – but the leakage spills truth   *(build)*
and the maniacs of power and money scream with
their backs against the wall – *one more year*
and the world turns hotter, the extremes war for dominance.
Democracy, which is a treasured ideal,
is fought tooth and nail, evil distorts the mind
of the ugliest people of all touting their own race
as God's backside, the only thing to sit down with   *(build)*
as they sit down with their white backsides on everybody else
and exert their craziness on their controlled media
one more year, and the resistance grows as the overlooked females
take over the podium, the greater half of suffering Earth
exerts to be proud and the genius form of democracy   *(drop to*
spreads to everyone left sane – *one more year* and the   *quiet)*
exotic frequency of love sounds out, breaks through,
the treasured vote grows in demand of sanity.
Compassion arises rising through common sense,
the value of a new country birthing democracy
radicalizes the need for cooperation – one more year
is all you need, we need, it's coming *one more year.* /20Jun2018

DeKooning Buddhism

A masterpiece of in, of of, of in step with time
    sliced to flat
color in infinite defining of itself caught in
    cooperative/individualistic stance
prayer inflow of breath, breathe ever so lightly,
you think on point but don't dance on point
a relaxed point of thinking, not thinking the view –
winning wonder down to topple Earth into itself
as breadth, height collapsed into canvas cover
color - what is the notion of now but all over the place.

Secretly I Love Openly

Secretly I love openly
and to be ever astonished I can't be.
I can't be anything if I'm nothing
with my heart *in* my heart and never
on my sleeve.
Quiet times cover the screaming
but age subdues what can't be subdued.
Opposites go on around the clock
letting everything out that stays within
where it stays – love at long last love,
correct in any name if it is pure,
part of nature and an unknown known,
known to be the light that warms and lights
where no one sees better than I do.
You can love just as much as you can't
as I do, who would know anyway what I know,
burning everything into a joy, or is it was it
can it be?

Known To Be Known

Known to be known for who you are
may not be what anyone can be,
the perfectly open man not perfect at all,
not open, even puzzled in all his clarity.
The puzzle takes over that can't be played,
figured out can only end with a confused
surrounding while the inner potency continues
without a doubt as if anyone knew about it.
They all do within themselves, every one
without fail succeeds in having that unclamped
secret known openly, ever present to yourself.

The Mind Carries On Love

The mind carries on love as if it truly exists
that is, palpably, a one on one occasion
in real life, bleeding souls, healing and renewing,
but mostly love rides the day being the underpinning
of every movement, rudimentary or significantly
powerful – and it is the carriage of the mind that
reminds the body through every ride bumpy or smooth
through the day. There is no substance to love
at all, when it isn't there before you in your hands
in your eyes and hearing and embrace.
It is a driving force coming in and out of
an obsession of the mind. Oh yes, love exists
in your imagined formulations when
a person you love is far away, or even gone forever.

Pray(se)

For rain
for the gardens in it
for remembering to boil the pasta al dente
for the potato salad
with the potatoes boiled just right so
they don't fall apart
for the water in the cat's dish she wants
placed in the bathtub so
she can jump in and get it when she wishes,
for washing the lettuce keeping
the water in a pot underneath for watering the plants
for that quick shower including washing the hair
for drinking that cool drink with some ice,
for the morning coffee, for the espresso in my case
for the dishes washed clean and clothes clean in those
    fancy new water conserving machines,
for the water pumped onto moistening pads
    of our swamp cooler on the roof
and the ability to flush the toilet with that precious
    1.6 gallon flush
for water to wash the hands and brush the teeth
    comb the hair
splash my face in the morning,
for the plants, the water that keeps them alive
both inside and outside, especially the fruit trees
cherry apple pluot apricot and the pines
taller than a house and, new, the baby ponderosa
for everything our lives have stood for in
the garden after garden after garden
with rows of lettuce cabbage broccoli green beans
tomatoes, jalapeños, corn, butternut squash
now long gone, as irrigation of the wonder of wonders
dwindled year after year –

for rain, the sensible gift of the Earth and
    building clouds
the moisture in the body, the lingering moisture in the air

for rain that makes good sense in the rolling evolving
      nature of things
for the Earth undamaged and respected by its inhabitants
the roiling atmosphere and cycles of cycles of seasons,
for rain, the touch and smell of it on Earth, kiss
      to the dry dirt
to empower refresh revitalize seeds and suffering native
      plants
for rain in the hot persistent days into weeks the heat
      spell
the dry killing atmosphere, the water table in levels and
      fractures
sinking far below us
for rain and the gardens in it, the life in it above below
in every direction the need coming out of it in
      suffering times, praise, the need to flow in cooperation
            of all elements
for rain again and again
      the gardens of Earth in it
life dependency refreshed
the power of the thunderclouds responding
out of the growing need, the given refreshment
satisfying all Earth thirst,
water as it is known to happen
in desert, in mesa mountain juniper piñon
as everything is looking up
for rain restoring the creek and filling
the deep crevices,
for the gardens in it
the water ways the water in it
presently
praise.   /30June2018

Oh Aurora

Male prominence is the sky darkening –
equality is a no-no to the prick crowd.
Swallow every supreme with genitalia.
Crow cock and all cock and cockamania.
Cock a dude'll do, throw another guy in there
with addled thinking, eyes too close together and a prick
    to tease.
You got your jock on, talk it out and fart dominance.
Evil is as evil does, you better walk the talk
and pat each other's back as you jack up your bank
and make sure the universal coinage has a testicle on it.

Arms race wins every time as the oligarchy gags on
the self-effete. Bravo hate-spitter dominating fellow bastards
bringing the all-punched-out carcass of manhood
back to life again with joy-juice of high-class whores
and paid deception, cruelty crippling the nation,
the sphere of Earth boiling in your pot of ignorance.
You can't get any worse with your fist first,
your pants down as you shit on democracy,
rub elbows in each other's autocratic faces
and in private foster deals to enrich your asses.
All things pass as time locks you in your own tentacles.

The female weight of Earth rolls over and crushes you –
the furor of your fat domain explodes like a blimp
    of hot gas –
the livid lies of your hate dissipate, turn
    in on its sick self,
the people of ordinary power grow against you
and shame slashes your union of dominance.
Humility itself stands more powerful
as any of your flag-waving stupidities
    and cheat-to-win mentality –
common sense brings an equilibrium that cracks
    egomania like
a million ants crawling up to bite your balls
    and balance as an act of peace sways you back

to the pipsqueak your heavy handed dominance
    brought yourself down to, it flows down, it
changes, it covers and surprises, it puts
the knife back in the scabbard, the shout back in silence,
billions of voices allowing an ancient song to sing.

    Oh aurora
    oh world
    gift of Nature
    a hand to hand
    oh known time
    a balance of sexes
    sings again a gain
    to all. /13Jul2018

In The Valley

    Know men
    but keep to Women.
    Be in a valley of the world.
    By being in a valley
    your true self will not desert you.
    You will enjoy the innocence of a child.

    Be conscious of the white world
    but favor the black
    all colors of the world, your model.
    Being the good example
    you have eternal power
    in the simplicity
    of all your beginnings.
    Be honored by true humility –
    be the valley of the universe.

Get It Right With Him

I would if I could of
but wouldn't instead
since not is not no
and no no-no is not necessarily
not, would could & should
not be not could, but never *no* means
as sometimes known to everybody
him and me are the same, him me
me him because we are equal
in the power game of no meaning not maybe
but *always* is as we say
as I say what it is always what it is
what he says makes more sense
then anything I say, what he says I say
so I should have said he told me
what I know to be true which is
everything he says is what I do

no, no I didn't say I said
what I really mean or meant to say
no when I say no means nothing
as nobody knows what we said when
we turned the world on its ass in private
so stick it up your no no I said
I do to him he said you do-do
what I buzzed into your ear
via translator to do, stand up
click your heels, bow, no that's not
what I said that is what I meant
I said you get it wrong you always
get it wrong just get it right with him
I mean me me him. /19Jul2018

US is the Underbelly of U.S.

I give up to the secretions of life
the avalanche of power man withstanding
the secret trades in the pus market
in the Hotels of Hypocrisy where ugly deals
make the bloated scabs more rich.
The sick elite are beyond my reach
not that I want to touch their poison.
I give up to what I can do, do nothing
but raise the creative healing with pure air
flowing and the sun knocking the clouds out
to reveal you and me that's all there is together
in this co-op of the seasons where our commonality
frees the bonds of capitalism leaning back
on the tilt of the world's Nature-positive power.

Unstuck

This is it
it ain't going away.
We're stuck with it
as it sticks to us
so maybe it will grow off
fall off with time.
I know it won't heal
but maybe it will descend
with its heaviness
as we slither out
free, free as I want to be
and truly am.

Here We Are

Has a long time passed that you could gain anything from a poet?
Have you heard anything from a poet with ears.
Is there music in them words?
What is the message, is the message in the music?
Is it just shouting and vainglory, let's hope not.
Does the younger poet seek out the older?
Is the concept of poet dated and done with.
Has wacky politics and the morbidly wealthy stamped out poets?
That is, any relevance a poet could have in a country of obese
    falsehood?
Has the lack of reading also increased the lack of hearing?
Has poetry become personal therapy only.
And not only that, has it died on the societal bush?
Is the flower dead, passee, the music that kept the doors to great past
    voices drifted down silent?
Has meditation absorbed poetry into the sound of crickets and
    an infernal ringing of the ears?
Does concentration turn into a concentration of the wits
    a concentration camp where dead voices listen to
        each other, only?
Has the poet's speech been taken away, neither free or prescribed.
Has Corporate World squeezed every living art out, as if it never
    heard a poet's voice at all.
Has the planet itself given over to its own global changes in response
    to irresponsible human damage
and where does that leave poetry or the arts or museums or libraries
    or scientific academies or universities too expensive to attend
        and possibly encourage or bring in contact a body
            of work of a poet, great voices of
the 20th Century into the 21st Century buried in the debris of human
    ignorance and millions of petty survivalists
as the Warlords, rather, World Corporations, war with waves of
    refugees in every nook and hollow and
war against all the new walls just built to keep people somewhat
    different apart?
I think embracing the local can open a voice here and there to hear,
    honestly hear our way out of this.

So what if you feel alone and your teachers and friends, poets
        almost all, have died.
In geologic time this is almost nothing. In a spirit of cooperation
        voices can be heard, mass changes empowered by youth.
Music may save poetry, coming out of the young, as more and more
        take to writing it down, learning it, expressing it.
Cooperative publishing adventures, music in language transformed
        to music in poetry, national, international grid of voices
refuse to be silent, as it always will like the spring, like the dawn
        like new species proliferating out of world change,
meditate on death in the past and rise up renewed as
what is that unusual voice, the eternal use of the muse, the open ear
        to music again and again, the uninhibited beauty.
What was lost was never lost as refinding finds, beginnings
found all over again. Singing never stops singing somewhere
sometime, the beauty of the found image as each new image
        is found
and expressed and the music of hearing voices pull out of the future
which is the astounding present, pressuring forth. Is there music
        in them words?
What do you think? Where have you been? Here we are.

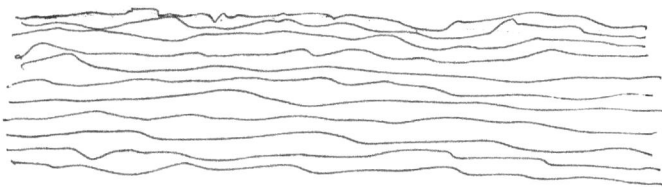

Healing Time

    Nature is in cahoots with time going by
    to heal, both working together,
    or if there is no time Nature meets up with now
    in all its mystery and healing takes place
    on the mend, the body-mind-spirit treasure
    of life. Time will tell, get well.

Nature Itself

    Christians of hatred & fire
    who've gone to the edge of an upside-down Christ
   you've turned into your twisted fate
  exerting megachurch control over others –
 your prismatic leaders have exchanged water for money
to do your baptisms in, vats of untaxed
that goes to the top bosses and for propaganda wrenched from sense
into self-righteous ego control jamming your tentacles
 all the way to the Supreme Court like an octopus of hate
  forcing your will on others as far from any God's will
   as it can be, destroying separation of church and state
    forcing women to birth the unwanted and unplanned,
     crucifying the Constitution on your cross –
      God save us from your godless God
       you created out of the dungeons of feudal clansmanship,
      extrapolating your Mammon from Jesus's antithesis –
     what happened to love in your altars of pelf
    sacrificed to your evangelical money god.
You are your own selves, diamond studding your pastors
and hanging Jesus's care for the unfortunate and sick
out to dry, far far far from the doors of your church,
 the prophet of love locked out from your profit of selfishness
  and know-it-all ugliness – the burning glare of control
   fuming from your eyes – away and out and enough –
    the spirits of love and truth are not in your transplanted religion,
     the ancient beauty of native ground has spoken here
      long before you forced yourself on it, killing its residents.
     Listen as the Earth truly speaks of love and diversity above all,
     open-mindedness and commonsense commonality.
    Nature voices Nature voices, care and healing as dawn
   comes out of the mess of your making night as strictured as
  a bed of nails, so welcome the dawn of compassion & tenderness,
 the moon and the stars and the Earth, what more do you need?
All we are is caretakers   of this vast gift.   /1Aug2018

    "Truth is something so noble that if God could turn aside from it,
        I could keep to truth and let God go." - Meister Eckhart

America's Problem

The nuts have popped their bolts. All across the country hardly anything works. Monkey wrenches are out of stock everywhere, and pliers, even tweezers. Fingers are blistered from useless twisting. Even electronic equipment has fallen apart, bridges collapsed, buildings unsteady. No one can get around as cars have stalled, trucks immobilized, jet planes grounded.

President Balloonface met with President Puke'n since Puke'n's Secret Mafia Service developed new tech to unscrew all the bolts of the world big & small. But Balloonface's buddy, Puke'n, says they *haven't* used it on America, oh no. So President Balloonface returned home convinced his candyass buddy Puke'n is not to blame. What is America to do with all our bolts undone? Our nuts free to roam useless and unscrewed?

2018 Etiquette

Avoid face to face contact at all cost.
Do not talk to anyone in person.
Do not land-line phone anyone.
You may email one line only.
but you may text and emoji at will.
You may Twit and Facebook Message
and Instagram. Damn it!
Avoid eye contact.
Keep your face down to phone.

Gentle Rain

What beautiful light can hold the candle to you
as the rain hits the roof late at night –
what sun comes into your life and shields from darkness
as its preciousness is most sacred
blackish clouds the background to everything
as thunder announces announces –
what dancing is done for you behind your back
beyond your sight some feet are hitting the ground
as the drums thunder change
as the voices you can't ever hear are there
doing their patterning with the drummers and bells and dancers –
what beautiful locality supports even when you transport your
    foreign ego on it
what beautiful people have been here before us
as the seasons were their panorama and the piercing stars –
what world of wildlife ran free as the buffalo, the wolves
    and even the far jaguars
as the same sun gave direction and the moon and stars
    to the lone hunters and communal farmers.

What respect as great as the Earth itself have you pushed aside
everyone, all of you, all of us
to inhabit trophy trucks and vacuous houses
to straw water out of the Earth with no thought of replenishment.
When the rain comes now, the kiss of night gift
that could be so rare as not to come, *not to come,*
who gives *thanks* or just says *not enough*?

There's never enough when all we do is take –
what earth has had enough? is it *our* Earth?
What planet are we on, that knows what we are doing to it –
is it our planet as we cover up its ancient voices
that warned us of greed, the poison of lying
    the tottering destruction of self righteousness
the leaning toward ignorance so we can have our way?
The way of extraction with poisonous chemicals
burning our way up into the atmosphere to

help heat our planet to extinction?
What is the soft message of this gentle rain that has been so rare?
It is the song of Nature singing just what it is if I listen,
what is there to hear in this gentle rain that is so rare.   /Sep2018

Curiosity

Words take me to a union I never had.
Two brothers holding hands.
One has no brother.

No Nada

                    In a time of this in holes
                a vacuum of deceit
            conniving in a post-Reagan amplification,
        he, towering, fell into himself
      all over himself
     under and around himself
   until himself was as zero as a vacuum –
he was a disappeared entity of gas
of non-gas, of non stinky gas –
              he was a fleshless blimp
          an invisible smoke –
      he was gone like a ray gun – gone gone gone,
    a "nattering nabob" of non-negativism –
he was a nil, a naught.
  As your Bone Daddy said, he was zilch
zip, nada, a diddily-squat, an ought.
  Ought he do nothing if he wasn't there or anywhere –
    he was a squatting down to pee when there was no earth
      to squat on, no pee, no reason to squat
    since he was the man he wasn't –
  he was emptiness a blank a nix a nihility
an oblivion, a scratch out, a zippo
  a buffoon without the buff or the oon
    a goose egg, a zot, a nullity
      a void without the *v*, the *o*, the *i*, the *d* –
        he was a nothing, a no no, a thingless non-thing –
      he was what he deserved to be –
        aghast at his non self
his puncture-less puncture of reality
  a fabrication without fabric,
    a triviality without existence –
      and people *went about their business*
        starting to do things again
          since there was no trace of him
            no fly, no speck
              no nada, no nothin'
                no *poof.*

From Memory

Let it go as they all say and hardly any do.
Hanging on to the precipice and not falling
is more than difficult, almost impossible.
And yet just saying "Let it go" can backtrack
to a time when it wasn't such a problem.
Maybe a fantasy of sanity that reassures
by accomplishing the impossible.

※

"To thine own self be true" as if I'm two people
lecturing myself, correcting myself.
Now Larry, you know who you are or do you?
Don't pull the wool over your own eyes.
See with clear vision for once, things as they are.

※

Do not impose God on reality which is composed
of energy components far beyond your imagination.
Let reality speak for itself and teach you
all you need to know.

※

One day at a time is the only way to be
at one with the day
to allow the dawn to begin you
the noon to middle you
the evening to mellow you
the night to complete you.
As it is with the planet
providing you.

※

Don't take yourself too seriously.
There is a rule that's one time too many
throw it out for simplicity.
Or if there are many many
throw many out indubitably.

Youthful Gain

What is more important to be said than what isn't said,
that I tell you that I love you silently, and make my living amends
without complaint, that I do what I do, you may not appreciate
as none of us gets as much praise as we think we deserve.
Time secretly passes all the time and the wonders of the Hubble
    universe dwarf us.
I speak for myself – the human ego if left unchecked will destroy
    the Earth.
Getting to help others helps myself and little by little even the rich
    will hear
how they can't continue on their path of greed and inequality
and if they do billions starve but we each can educate others with
    our quiet love
love in action silently grows in the youth coming forward
    everywhere.

Leaving Roswell

The flat plains of nowhere become somewhere when you look
    the cotton, the maize, the alfalfa
and the city of conveniences set up by cooperation and commonality
but it doesn't take much to stretch beyond into unwanted territory
for most people there, nice people who remain unstretched.
So the art in your head, the music in your hands,
the creative fire in your heart moves you *out of there*
when the time comes at last when you know the world of
unpatented discovery calls you to the big city, the university,
the layout of books, records, people, courses, city adventure,
the unknown tickling you with what can be known,
a universe of extensions so far from where you were,
so far leading you to where you are,
to be part of a three dimensional world of unlimited imagination
    created.

Dumb Fuck

He touches the goat with his lips and says
"You are a cow."
He runs his fingers through his hair and says
"Gold in them hills."
He puts his tie on backwards and reveals
    dried jism.
He's the cock that crows with hardly a cock and
    despiser of crows.
He laughs heartily without a heart.
He picks his audience and cheers to jeers outside.
He destroys facts by nailing them to the
    coffin of his father.
He leaked his urine and blamed the FBI.
He doesn't give a fig about figs or giving.
He knows he's king and knows it by not knowing anything.
He can con anyone but truth seekers who he calls liars.
He stokes the fire of his adherents by being the goofball he is.
He's the incarnation of the rip-off and the Judas of dumb
    Christians.
He gleams like gold and pays others to remove the mold
    under his skin.

Absent

Hollow beast
    are you alive in your deadness?
How do you live in your skin
    when it has been molted
        years ago?
Living on a lie is more than balancing on thin ice,
    it's plunge into-the-pit-of-your-own-falsehood
        to be there *alone*.
Everything you touch turns into
    your own thin skin –
not even a toddler, a baby –
    a sperm with no tail
and nowhere to go.

Judge Brat And
The Year of the Man

I keep my face scrunched up into a denial of everything
pinched around the suck ass nose splotch of alcohol.

How can I be guilty?
I may be *accused* of lots of things –
child laundering, teenage baggage
abandonment of the mind
little excessive flirtations,
but I'm never convicted of the *biggies* –
big moneyed magnates will take care of that.
It's the corporate donor period –
I'll bless you with my return of favor.
I'm a backbone Catholic - birth control free -
look at what our priests can do,
abuse is nothing to many of them
    my saints
once a choirboy always a choirboy,
innocent till never proven guilty.
I'm an adult, remember,
nothing matters except what I say is so.
Lock a woman in a confessional booth
    where she belongs
and me, I prefer an upper bedroom.
Hold 'em down and get what you want
and hide behind a blackout, oops!
Don't mention that.
I never did what I did and continue to do it.
I never attended the gatherings I attended.
It wasn't vomit I vomited when
I never over-indulged, got aggressive
and didn't do things I did.
Senator Hatch, Senator McConnell
Thank you all, Whitest Malest Men Buddies.
It's truly, and I kid you not,
the Year of the Man. /4Oct2018

Judge Brat's Notes

Us boys will be boys and girls are to be used.
Discount locker room talk.
They're not their bodies but ours.
Men run the sun, we are the true light.
Lie with efficiency.
Any accusations throw back with unrelenting
force to the accusers.
Annihilate.
Morality is on our side.
Turn everything to profit
in the Court of Eternity.

Anal Party

Republicans are anal to oral.
They reduce everything to the backside of history.
They shove their corporate backed ass
into everyone's face.

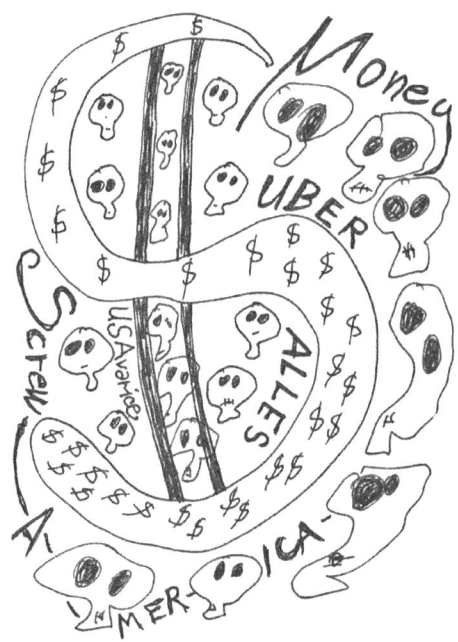

Guiding Eyes

Light of the guiding eye
that sees what I don't see,
bring the morning fruitful
in what I see and do,
as one can only follow
an honest inclination.

Solo Dancer

They'll never find out the hiding on my part
the concrete presence of reality
because it isn't concrete,
but staring you in the face relentlessly.
Did our fantasies explode into true light,
our passions un-arm themselves
and jump off towers, any place high
usually avoided, us with them?
The burning sensation of that light
seen through an invisible prism, holds.
Dancing, singing, erupting vocals
when least expected.
What's wrong with the dance when
no one else is dancing, but not with yourself
but with the energies that prevail
bursting out.

On Laboring at Meditation

Isn't there an easier way to do nothing.

Rescue Next To You

What is the percentage of rescue for my heart?
I think it is zero although the dial is not
locked on that –
starved to the end of time the hungry
who live even full lives or can,
but not the fullest.
But then whose is fullest.
I doubt if secrets are ever revealed –
the gift comes as grace,
the rescue comes so near it excites the imagination
and nearer to God am I –
someone is brought to me in the guise of rescue
almost – someone doing a job,
someone interested in one of my interests
that the possibility of a friend is refreshed,
that opens the heart it comes so near,
and then someone dies or goes away.
Humanity is starved, let's face it, or rather,
let's not face it.

First One

It broke my heart to be the first one to have
	his heart broken.
Oh what a measure of suffering to come.
This just defies description. It's just a suffering through.
Oh suffering, someone has to invent it.
Unreturned love is the worst or is it
	painful hunger?
It's been so long I can't remember.

In Good Hands

It'll get out of hand if you hand it over to a cruel hand.
They're waiting in the shadows to dust your future with disaster.
And then you cough and come down with lung rot.
Or simply die untended with cancer or simply die unattended
    with cancer.
Healthcare is a right and not a privilege of the privileged who have no
    interest in your rights and would assume you have none.
For isn't it a club as they try to get to the club of the club of the clubs
and more of them make it while the earth of everyone, what we used
    to call the masses,
are their debris, for their wealth must be strangled out of something –
mainly you and me, the cocksie Koch's are clueless about what's
    going on.

Their think tanks can be run by only so many people – they forget
    the bees
yes the busy bees of persistence, dedication perseverance passion
insistence, millions of little bees the whole alphabet of resistance
for what is right, common sense, commonality, non-party insistence
    on the good
the eruption of care, yes, care for others, not do as thou wilt
but do unto others what you would have them do unto you
or have you forgotten, you stupid you, with all your brains narrowed
    into conniving
you forget the bees, we bees work together and we butterflies, you
    forget the butterflies –
we're in flocks and we can move great distances as well as be
    beautiful at home –
you forget the wolves, hey we're growing in numbers
and we're good predators for preserving the balance of nature
and you idiot buffoons in your gold-plated pantaloons
forget all the migrating birds, we move openly and mysteriously
    great distances following the patterns of nature –
have you heard of the patterns of nature, have you even heard of
    Nature?
I didn't say despoiling, I didn't say poisoning, corrupting,
dominating destroying raping exhausting, misusing, fraking and
    generally fucking everything up
I said patterns of Nature, Nature undominated but cooperated with
the Earth itself presents solutions – Nature, Mother Nature,
    Father Sun
the Moon Magician and the Universe of Stars Galaxies of Higher
    Powers
cockeyed cockamania corporations of calculated accumulation
massive power of the few, you few are few – watch out for the ants
the ants working everywhere millions and millions, ants here
ants there, ants everywhere crawling up your legs to bite
    your you know what and you can't stop us we're at the
polls we're in the voting polls, we're better known as the populace –
we're everything you've ever not wanted to happen
and sooner or later your manipulating the vote gets overwhelmed
with the rush and flood and tsunami of the popular, who really won
    the last election?

We more than exist – we sing, we create, we make scientific
 discoveries
we do business with everybody, we're every color of the rainbow and
 then some
we're into the commons and we demand that the billions going into
 the military be accounted for, heard of public accounting?
Not for greed & war, but for good
and the millions going into our common needs be encouraged in
 schools, government, roads bridges internet education – and *fun*
till the commons is again common, and common sense prevails
teachers scientists artists respected
living wage workers' unions listened to, co-ops building, private
 business flourishing, green and all color industries prospering
sane laws kicking out assault weapons, national buy back of guns
 cutting violence and boosting mental care, law-abiding hunters
and fishers and conservationists valued, women's voices heard and
believed and the addictions to hate & drugs turning into addictions
 of compassionate love –

we *bees* we butterflies we birds we wolves
we *ants*, we native plants, we cooperative humans flowering,
we sunflowers along every road in America, backyards and fields,
not only are we along the roads, we're *in* the roads, driving and walking
 colorful attending, we the engaged populace standing up
everywhere turning away lies and celebrating truth
open minds bound to free speech, and separation of church & state,
every woman and man born equal under law & love
peace of mind and health of mind & body joining each and other
joining with civility, a new name in our honor – we might as well sing –
let freedom ring

Rainbow Speaking

The light at the end of the world
    at the bottom of the pit of longing
progresses through the memory of rainbows
    astonishing the real thing.

"I am what you bend out of
if only you know yourself
through the tricks of nature
a relaxing of outside tension –
Simplify Yourself!"

The demand meets impossible solutions
    till the light bends through itself
steady from the source
    and illuminates particles of water
floating in air.

Wealth Sickness

Don't disturb me with your miasma
your color utopia, your debunked paradise
your straightforward ascension has only tickled yourself.
Nobody but you laughs at your urine specimen –
it's purple and turns to red and defies analysis.
I've heard your plumbing is all rotted from your body issues.
Your house teetering on its billion dollar foundation.

Love Unfolds

Love folds itself in and keeps quiet
but unfolds in the presence of the loved.
Like a sea flower, an opening primrose
or opening lips.
The unfolding to the loved
is the most beautiful thing in the world.

Exactly the Same

Welcome to obverse, reverse, perverse
where everything is normal, abnormal, subnormal.
We work and play where we do nothing every day,
vote our consciousness, or whim, our negative reactions
to every positive thing – we are prepared for everything
    nothing, something, some things are just
not to be stated so I will tell you all about it –
the ups, the downs, the middles, the true dope and the lies.
Obviously I'm a spokesman, a know-nothing
    a silent nincompoop, the smartest man in the world,
a creature of habit original in every word, never repeating myself –
repeating myself is verboten – did I tell you or did you intuit
I never repeat myself, only others, I'm a complete re-representation
of yourself since no two people could be more opposite, in color,
in degree, in background, in expertise, in singing ability and
    in human grace – you and I are the same as she is, also
totally different from you and me as we are in complete
    contradiction
and she and I have become one, one of two opposites exactly
    the same.

Ever Present

"The quality of the imagination is to flow and not to freeze."
- R.W. Emerson

Obviously if you focus on the real, the real comes to life and a life of living is worth your while while you carry on as if nothing is happening, everything is. That is, as it is happening it carries you along with it. Snap your fingers and the dancing girls appear, it's that simple. Oh, they are dancing women. Now they are men. Do you see what I mean. I have taken you over. *You* have become a control freak. A control pervert. A wrong shoe on the right foot. And something to be desired on the left. Watch the left, it's the right side of your brain.

What you think is to not think at all. Politics is like a cushion to sit on. Sit down. Sit down on it and don't let it wriggle around. You are your own King, the Queen of your King. You decide what you have done. *Now* presses on into the future which you'll never know. Everything evolves but time. Just go with it as if you have a choice. Your choice is to not choose. Although you can fight Ennui like the French masters did. As they got bored their poetry froze. Continue to be a hot number but don't think you know how to lead. You're a born follower, at your best. Open your ears, shut your mouth, listen to what's not worth hearing or hear what's not worth listening to and you'll be the divine prince of all time, or some of the time or maybe not divine and actually not a prince but just an innocent individual not so innocent after all as you face your faults raining down around you – nothing is perfect including yourself. Your self that is not your "I" as "I did this" "I am" since you have no idea what your "I" is and yet you're as palpable as anybody else – your prayers are breathing, your heart beat is your lust for life, gratitude fills every boat you set sailing from your mind. Thoughts that set their streams on wings. Calculating forward, calculating backward. Life, Tao, anyhow, what's flying now, flying out from your dreams. Your bungling self is not in the way for a change, you've read some masters of the mind and soul, what is soul, is it soul-delicious? Something you can eat, digest and perfect? Or is grace ever present?

As if you can force anything. "Man ahead" you say, *Knock* it into place. Hammer the soul into some prescribed shape. Just try it just like Dr. Johnson lashing the wind to get it to stay still – language grows through your fingers, it's wild, you can't stop it or why should you try? You know good and well you have something to say and nothing to say if you truly *listen.* Slice the wound rubber bands of a golf ball with a sharp razor blade and they spring free, you're suddenly unwound, you relax, easy does it, as all your clamps explode, your vices loosen, your Vice-Grips pop open, as empty as all those water containers you emptied out, the outward of you is connected to the inner, a giant zero, a nothing a sense open sensefulness, a relaxed *oo* and *ah*, willing and ready to receive or open to the nothing that is there which is liberated by your own silence.

What is there is everywhere as long as it doesn't go to your head. What head, the head on your shoulders, or my head. Who am I anyway, as if saying something is *my* prerogative only. You better shut the fuck up, or I better shut my mouth having said all I have to say about receiving grace, not Grace Kelly, not Grace Atkins but plain ole grace, like a lovely tiara for men as well as women or a circle over the head, but not an old-fashioned halo, not a glowing. A lifting without wings, a commitment out of self, self annihilated under the dancing feet, the game of dance, the dance of a game where everybody wins. That is its nature as your feet touch the ground, why shouldn't they, walking hiking exploring returning sitting lying down with feet up. Behold it's time to sleep, don't you think it's about time to give it up, release, let go as they say, isn't that the secret all too obvious, now ever present for everybody?

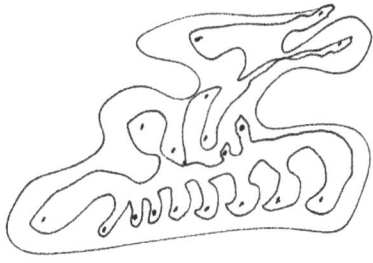

Wishful Thinking

Since the Muse has abandoned me
    I have to fabricate it,
        take the US and put inside of
    ME,
        MUSE.
I am a US citizen,
    a muse of another color
        but could be the same.

Belled Out

At the sound of a bell
my mystical consorts play around my cranium
my left side says hello to my right side
my upside incorporates my downside
my center expulses ignominious goo
and I'm free to play around with my freedom
happily chanting "I love you, you bilious baboon you."
Suddenly I'm in the jungle, the jungle of repentance
everything about me is a swollen apology
and my insignificance treads before your elephantine perfection
how can I ever breathe the same breath as your exhaled golden air.
Yes, at the sound of a bell I've become the nothing ranted about
by the oriental Saints of Vacuumhood.
I'm attenuated into the finest tissue spread around the world
three times
and I disappear. Thank you marvelous bell, for nothing.

They All Have Mothers

These masculine gods no matter where they are,
and as far back as they go, all have mothers,
predecessors from whence their presence is born.
So what is it – Father or Mother – it is both
in the knitting presence of matter even the plus and minus
the give and take, push and pull all the way back
to the big bang of out-of-nothing-something.
So don't give me this "Our Father" shit.

Bye Bye Dogma

Incarcerate your dogma and walk away
free as the world.

As The Stars Tell

As the stars tell all
you open your mouth and let them talk
does a fire produce fire out of nowhere?
Is the magic the true beginning?
Is the beginning now in the dark?
What stretched out of nowhere, somewhere?
We will find out by peering into our past.
Give good thanks to the mechanics of science
for building the trappings to get there
to mirror our vision of the unknown
suddenly speaking like stars from our mouths.
"Oh did you want us to say something?"
                    /Winter Solstice 2018

Directions

The burning fires of my outraged heart
can't be quelled by this short-light day
but early morning with Venus on the rise
will tell another story, another turn
as we all work instead of wait
to return and make anew good sense,
the songs of earth choirs
determining our directions
directions north south east west
anywhere.

Inflated Doodad

"At war with principles
I stagger on into
non-running realities.
It's as if my spirit is frozen.
Everything cold but no snow
as if I cared.
What does nature have to learn
except from me
that is, a whisper is a shout
in my ruling world.
An inflated blimp
is my balloon brain. I am King God
or God King of
sweeping away
reality as you know it –
truth and all that business.
Give me a buddy hug
with an extended hand
held until you drop
and I win.
I win the game, the war
the board game –
hug all the chips to me,
Baby.
And give me the girl
in the backroom
always the backroom
for sex and the ultimate
degree
for a hot-knee salad
a luscious paid-for caress
I mean grab bag.
I'm your playful piñata
beat me
let the ooze come out
and I'll destroy your attention span
by throwing a rubber greasy ball
any time you start to think twice.

I'm the master of divert everyone
    from common sense
        to get my fond riches
            no matter what.
                See there you thought I was true
                    until I spanked your principles
                what's that, drop the foreign words –
            a turd is a cloroxed turd
        and you better believe what I say is
    your fountain of youth
your Shangri-la
your tiddle little squeeze toes
pad my foreign accounts
anything to accumulate
the dodo of doo-doo
    do you get what I mean?
        If you don't you're powerless
            in non-corruption.
                Tower up is tower out
                    tower in every place
                        chock full of glittering gold
                            toilets and portraits –
                                who's next in the Man Nugget
                            of the Year
                        the best pussy on the squeeze box
                    but make way for
                the ultimate chair – Me Myself and I –
            sitting there
        giving birth to little greed babies
    all over the world. "   /22Dec2018

Open to Secret

Your magnificence, your cosmos, your worlds beyond, your state of creation, of uncreated, the back hand of history, the mirror image of yourself exploded into rainbow intensity, magnified bursts through lenses countering sight as empty as all get out, outside of wonder awe-full and dark as black as regions of unfound blackness extended into millennia, stretched and restretched as light devours light, light empties out light, cosmos the opposite of chaos, the chaos of cosmos, as the unknown expands into the known, all-knowing known, leaps beyond the brightest star into the unformed, the reverse formed, the egg-shaped, the oblong, the huge to include everything, spectacular light displays, fiery creation mists opposite aurora-tested curtains of enveloping curtain, spread out surrounding and including, your reverence, your chemical concordance, your gain on gain on gain sucked through, accumulated, and ever, eternity added to your additions in multiplications of energy sources applied, re-applied, coming out of, out of days nights backwards collapse, broadcast telepath rhapsodic starcast, proliferating universes of cosmoses of thee, penetrating extracting gravitational pull, release charges recharged in multidimensional glow on glow on glow of you, of your destruction of whole power electric opposites into new newer entirely first foremost reaches to the end of reaches, reaching out to the innermost inner entertainment of the deepest, the devout double doubled deep in point of all time, timeless in nativity of you thee thou thou all in entirely embraceable line, solid matter maternity mode maddening madonna maitre master, minor plus minuses, molecular building evolution of evolving nature into maturity, infantilized fantasy grounded, sky bolting up out, free singing, forever dawn knighted brightened to your face of all planets, stars mother twin galaxies spiraling out, all spiraling in cyclical counterweight loss of outer space, magically pure science of inner space, your worlds beyond within you, your simply new new abreast of the old, all encompassing and surpassing your dancing, dancing out the play of neighbor by neighbor by neighbor, neighboring universe as present as the floor, ceiling, air of immediate compassion, intimacy of me talking to you, you listening as you are now, you to you from you from two and ones framing the heart that beats life into everything, you live living unmentionable wordless closeness, close ever near as far far far as near secretly open open to our secret, secretly open to our open secret open.

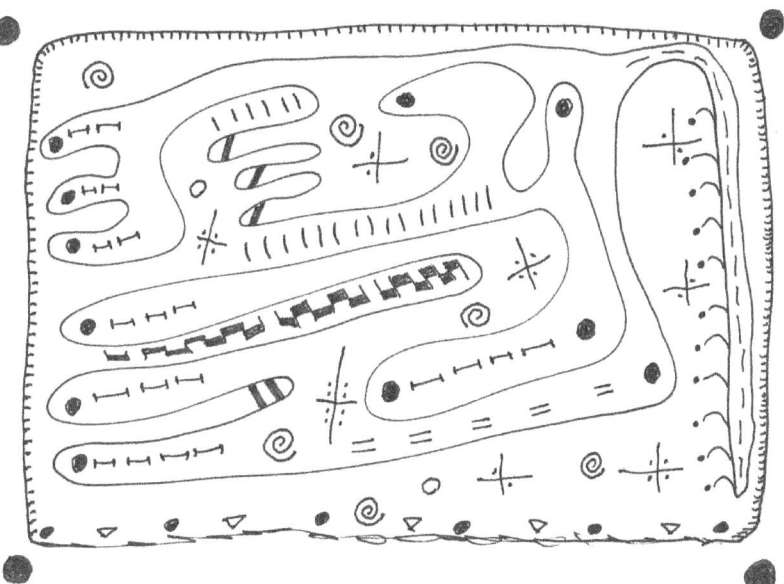

Queen Of Everything

Out of nowhere nothing arose in all her splendor.
She knew she was queen of everything because
she wasn't anywhere all at once.

Less Rotten Happy New Year?

May this year be less rotten than last year.
May it actually progress in solving problems and helping people
  helping the surviving species, helping the Earth reachieve
    its natural stability.
May supposed friends among humans discover a true friendship or two.
May technology not suppress what's left of the human spirit as we learn
  the values of companionship and helping others work together for
    the benefit of all.
May greed not *progress* in its control but regress actually turning into
  service and humility.
May the tendency to think big, buy big and be big dissolve into
  creative reality where less is more and small is at last big.
May new leaders suffuse government with new ears that listen and
  havethe courage to transform a decay of will into action.
May truth which has been here all the time reassert itself as the
  sublime, the continual eye-opener where progress is possible.
May humans open their minds and give up trying to control others,
  learn to love without taking.
May liars cheaters and thieves who made the last few years so rotten
  face consequences of their criminality.
We accept with joy the grace of new day, a new year, a daily new
  beginning.

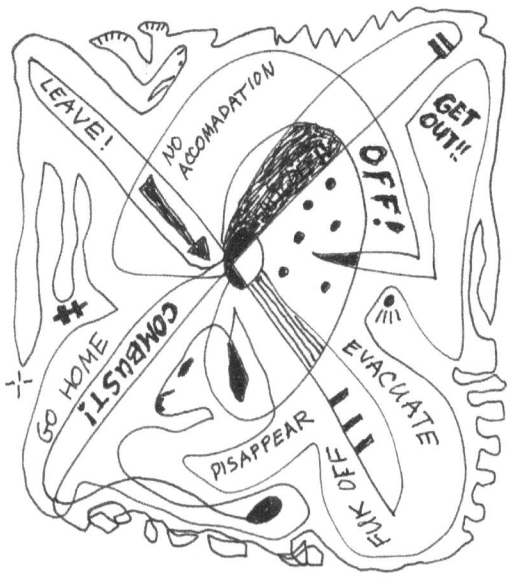

EARLY RISER
Poems - 2019

"I will imagine you Venus tonight
and pray, pray, pray to your star
like a Heathen. Yours ever, fair star."
      - John Keats (1795-1821)

Mother of Vast Decree

                Mother of Vast Decree
            "He shaped out of the wall a creature,
              a sort of half man, half woman."
         "Semele, mother of Dionysis, is the Earth ."
              "in her young form as maiden:
         rising out of the actual Earth she really is."
        She of the ground was probably at Olympia
              long before the coming of Zeus.
     Is there any recognition of spirit forming into god.
          A godless god or more god, a goddess
         an Earth destiny, a calling early morning
   out the door in the Southeastern sky the brilliant Venus.
           Having ascribed to something bright
       a destiny of one's own making or reflection of
           stirrings in Earth, an Earthling Earth
      Earth baby girl-woman he fashioned she fashioned
      the male-female fashioned caressed help lifted out
  of the Earth, Earth is and popped up all over the Planet.

    In restorative ages, ages old, of wild things she is native
    as nativity in all forms of Earth wherebouts unknown
       wherever you are settled down to the ground
           the old giving birth to the old again
         as to wherever you come to there was
             somebody there before you
 as before them there was somebody came to establish themselves
   where a woman, nameless, is overlooking a field she planted
          or the half-naked under the warm sun planted,
          the water spirits gushing in furrows.

Where you are now in giant houses overlooking the critical past
where have you come to to come out of it and refuse it and abuse it
the past follows you wherever you reject it.
Could it be the past was there before you and you
impose on it? That the new gods you bring are poison to
the old gods you build on and reject?

Who is you if not me, seeing the figure on the wall come to life
the old cracks and you fall into the cracks as I have
the crumbling walls of the recently washed through arroyo.

>   The dance of the seven veils could recently reveal her.
>   Struggling to draw you in dancing your youth away.
>   Origins speak louder than words.
>   Unveiled what was here before brought here
>   was here, stays here is here in recognition of quantum
>   Earth born out of what she is being, what she is rising from.
>   To thy power of her restablishment having never gone no place
>   having stayed as you are wherever you have come to.
>   Teaching the lesson of teaching the lessen of hearing.
>   What goes East again to come back having gone no place recently,
>   ear to the Earth, mouth closed to hear, eyes to what comes before
>   and hears what is there, not what was brought to bear heavily
>   on what is here, whose gods have already been in place, taken place
>   taken the place you hear or transport madness onto sanity.
>   Heavily dumping your new loudness on the quiet of this
>   early morning.

The dance is already here in the rural past, the respect of
scattered snow showers, of ache, of lack, of settling down into
hearing the quiet. A language or languages you'll never know
touching you what there is to know about where you are.

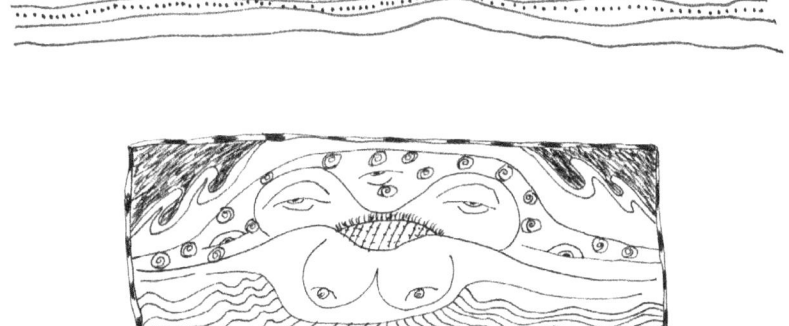

Do Not Give Up Playing Football

Mother of tired energy
do not give up playing Football
with old White Men.
Grab that ball and make your score.
All Colors fuse together to support you.
The cheering crowd goes home to revolutionize.

Walking On My Bones

Walking on my bones, heterosexual values exposed,
I run back to a fleshier time in my mind when
I didn't think of walking barefoot on the brick floor
as anything special, and if I did, I wouldn't have been
so aware of the jolt of bones as I walk on the slightly warm
floor – but that is the morning in a house with me and
my wife, after I discovered breathing and being aware of
my bare feet, walking.

Impossibly Blue

What am I gonna do I'm so blue
thinking of you or not you
but that there is no you.

Tufts

Look it up
and devour the innards of your grace
as if you have to work to find what's already there
living in the cave of your departure
awash from the millions out there
opening a book and pointing a finger
is haphazard hope
to break the barrier of isolation
"stones rolling around good for divining you know"
Oh voice from a voice of a voice
I don't fit in history because it's too cold to think.
Logic is lifting your voice to the snow.
Yes there is snow and a cold reminder
water has not abandoned us yet
here in mountain desert of yucca and prickly pear
and the rosettes of tufted evening primrose
already ready for the spring.

Loss Is Gain

A major part of life is loss
look at nature putting out so much
to get one germinating seed or none
millions of germinating seeds and all the seedlets
die in the frost.
And so it's such vast numbers of invitation to life
lost every day
I'm not going to strain, it can
take me with it in the rain
and I can dissolve like powder
giving up *trying* to let go is
the most refreshing letting go there is.

A New Leaf

Turning over, a new leaf, madness
turning over madness is what?
Non mad, un-mad, post mad
refused mad blotted, potted mad
mad done mad obliterated shot off in spheres of nothing
mad nowhere, no old mad either, no new mad
there is no mad, mad is mud, mad no mode
mad no more, no "m" no "a" no "d" together
no mention, no plot to reinvent, no move to recreate
restore bring back, matriculate, no way forward
for the backward despised, the tipping on total ruination
that was the mad before, a new day, a non mad day

no need to be mad anymore because the mad that was
is no more, no out-of-one's-mind, no crazy insane departure
from any common sense, no demented, perverse deranged
no tickling destruction and laughing stupidly foolish, abnormal,
enraged, furious, beside yourself, pure madness gone
goodbye rabid reckless, poisonous, gemaedde
gemaeded, no mad mudra, no mad before after, no mad now
turning over a new leaf, madness turning over reveals

a sane day, a day of soundness, a non-sad day
a day to repair, to go out and do, ever create along with relate
as it is happening, as it is happening today.   /16Jan2019

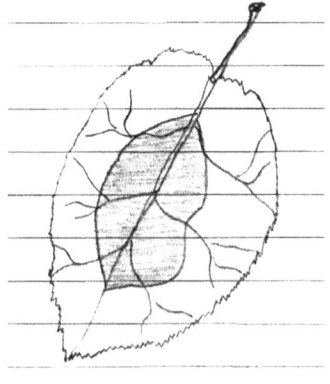

Spica They Tell Me

Straight up there in the timing of the stars . . . . .
Spica not looking down on anything just being
how can a star look down, how look, looking like
a picture book as if a book can picture oh you mean
full of pictures as the sky full of stars as if
nobody wants to look at them they remind them of the cosmos
oh cosmos what does our galaxy look like really, here in it,
how can we see it, we are looking various means all too
complicated when I don't even want to look up, to Spica
Virginis in Virgo, Spike - spike - ear of corn the
    Virgin is holding
it is not an ear of corn nor held by a Virgin, a Virgin not a Virgin
but still among the brightest 20 stars of what, our heaven
a heaven, not a heaven, but our viewpoint, a burning point in space
from our so limited point of view in this one little
    not little *to me* part of our galaxy such a tiny part of
the galaxy total, unknown total – a speck of light in my
limited sky and limited eye sight it's all
timing away stuck to time traveling, not really traveling,
I travel back to bed as the radio presents a Latin orchestra
of music not live but a disappearing segment of live musicians
some time ago, flute and drums, not a flute but a sound
not full orchestra drumming but a sound semblance.

I offer you an ear of corn although I'm not a virgin
and I certainly don't live in the stars and,
in fact, the fact is I don't have any sense of anything, really
as everything is *seeming* to be what it is.

That Humility

Christ is a brush with ego
where clear sight gains energy
and topples into the Godhead unintended.

Have I gone too far, the streaming light
says no, dizzying uncertainty vanishes.

And we're left with the questions
what did he really say, what struggle drew him to the fire
and saved him. What was his drawing power?

Was it love under oppression, a way out of misery?
A re-establishment of hope in something new.

Always something new eats at the old regime,
closes the door on the stubbornness of authority
as the care of others brings down the greed of some,
that humility that was almost lost at his death.   /11Feb2019

Beast

"What rough beast"
some ballyhoo monster
his head sticking out of his ass
comes to tootle his cheated victory
in the worst vision of a nation
a treasonous blow to democracy
this distorted afterbirth
of self-licking ego
surrounded by handpicked crooks
the worst assortment of sick sycophants
an entire party of the clan
of the white rich
coddling and lying for the buffoon
of privilege & deceit.

We Know Nothing

That we know nothing surprises
except the bad, those worst elements
that bite you in the face, but for now
there is a steady course towards love
or a stay there, it just infuses
the whole body, the receptive mind.

Dawn lifts up to awake and correct
to infuse back to all here in
this time zone, I have been absorbed.
It takes me, what? With it it
arises in me as your presence not far away
close, how close, how close can you get
to real love? I don't know what is real
but love simply appears with the day
in everything working together to play
at life, be life in love absorbing all so
it is care, a you and a me, what more to be
becomes "is." Let's find it playing out
together. Here this day, too near to miss.

Reflection of the Universe

I'll go in there and mother my god,
encourage her femininity and her strong will.
Who am I to do so?
A believer. I have faith in the Mother of us all,
the miraculous birth of the Universe,
all that pain to create and the joy of delivery.
Even if I project my humanness onto the screen
 . . . . of stars and galaxies
I get back an astounding chorus of yesses.

Mystery Caller

  Hone home a blessing
   as if I could give one
    let it come of its own accord
   ever without me
  but that rain of truth
 from mysterious origin
  softens the spirit
   and dampens the roots
    allowing growth
   may the energy of truth
  ever enter and calm
 ground you with
the love that aspires
to all things
 at their best
  giving the soul spirit
   the relationship warmth
    the family meaning
     built on trust
    all those big words
   dwarf me
  but I hear them
 resonating anew
as old things
  become new
   one time this time
    voice approval
    and some singing
    not mine but
    as in all things
     that greatness is out there
    and resonates
   in here in my
   proportionally tiny
   receptors
    just being open
   hearing going
  along with it
 peace that ritual
that is present as breathing
 that grounding
that come back to my
 senses firm grasp
  let go, the feminine
 refreshes spirit
in out
breath to be
 be as thou be
at best better
than best
  greets you as
   you pass it along
  to me
as always that
simplicity dissolves
debating and
refreshes tired spirit.

Who knows how far away
a responding and providing
friend unmet now
 deeply known
  sends the mysterious
  signal of acceptance
   consciousness older than all
   provides the harmony.
    Hello, glad to meet you
   that's exactly what
  I need and I need to
  pass on one to one
  to one to one
  simply an opening to it,
    what?
   It's unearthed, it's
   the deep down and
  far away as near.

Phenomena
   of simplicity
    that emptying out
    of pain and tightening up
  so that something
  more basic and less
   demanding slows
    the heart beat a bit
     and the breathing
    takes the mind
  with it
  unknitting the
    complexity that was
     the source of pain.
     That harmony hears itself
    harmonizing
   a better way is
  the best way,
  easier than thought,
   someone is telling me
    who is it from afar
     rooted in myself.

What To Do

Light enough to be light enough to be light enough
to be light enough –
lighten up.

Uh Oh

The Muse left me at the door
with no goodnight kiss.

Moralitee

"What is moral if it's not oral, or moon cow?
Hey baby, I like your tits, or mora*lu*city?
A tippled Gordon who's Gordon is he ordinary
faking his daughter's test scores, top-dollar lawyer
or a spoon fish? Any father would do it, family first, jerks.
Money stalks, the object of your fuckshun.
Why didn't the right and wrongers win?
Why do they always have to lead in the dark backwards.
I said I was blue and blew you out.
Your candle is no substitute for my finger.
Come quietly to come cheese
the best thing there is to bloat your meat with.
    Love your buns.
What is a gas turbine and how many do you have to import
before you change the racket, Washington must do your bidding
Why isn't Washington a city? It's a lobbyists' spa.
Suck it and you will, won't you, you're no good, bad mouth, get out.
My benefactors gave me 18 million denero to turn into poontang.
I don't bother with chicken Chicago or mortgage idiots
    who come from Mars. Don't bother me with details.
I want rough stuff behind the counter
    or the stage, desk of golden surprise.
Under the table, you little cutie, when I say shake you better shook
or I'll get my devil drawers to split open.
Luuuuve in the time of shit, peace in the time of blowhards
    and quadruple digit mayhem.
Back to the issue of morali*tee*, it isn't oral it's a twat squat
    to raise 10 billion dollars which is a chicken mattress compared
        to a moon pothole.
You know, when you're a kid & you have to ride in the limo
    by yourself
I hate that having to pretend not to cry – nobody makes me do
    anything.
Everything I have was given to me by the alley in back of Bergdorf
    Goodman, a little tete-a-tete with a corrupt state
corruption is my cologne, Chanel #69 prissy woman
I got your number you don't need mine.

Holiday for sparks and I've got electricity, the connection I need
to cross one country with another and end up with people turned
    into billions   of hard rock *cash*.
I mean I shouldn't have to do anything to lubricate the darn
    admiration pills – bow down and kiss-ass savvy.
We're talkin' bigtime when the belly button turns inside out.
Give everybody nothing and you'll have more to split
    your headache with.
You know the crotch is the brain part of success.
They're just dying to give every backside fantasized in a million
    years to you. Moi, baby.
So that's morali*TEE* which leaves little room for definitions.
It's there, you don't have to grab, you don't even have to squeeze
    to get the bottle off the top.
I mean is anything bigger than pleasure, being a bull in the China
    or any country's shop, nation, whoredom, oligarchal paradise.
I mean kill off the complaints, I'm talkin' firepower.
It's the massive itch of humanity but you know how to kill flies.
You know what I mean, scratch it, that's the moral thing to do.
Do 'um out of anything and park it between your knees.
What more do you got if you don't got everything?
    Think I'm kiddin'?
What's a little runt like you belly achin' you're not *gettin'* enough.
Your replacement's already kissin' ass.
You have a chance, but if you don't see it my way you're off
    the radar.
Duke it out you phoney baloney stony and get your own 2 dollar jar
    of Vaseline
a thousand tyrants in each bottle. Are you surprised?
My life is a gold dildo studded like a big stud with diamonds on top.
Cart those fuckers out! It's time to elope with madness."

I Couldn't Lie

I remember one day thinking
I couldn't lie, not just wouldn't,
that somehow it would violate
my very essence of being.
If you don't lie think what a
precious good person you are.
And what a practical good asset
    that can be in love, in friendship
    in just self reflection
    and open evaluation
    and shouldn't we all
    be so?
    Isn't a good feeling
    something sustaining
a healthy character
a dependable being
a reliable maybe even
useful human
capable of
a partnership of love
with even another even
    a society of friends
    based on the truth
    of interrelationships.
    What is better, ever, or is there
    anything better than truth?
    A reliable relationship with
    the universe, as it is?

My Derriere

The Christians came to kiss my ass.
Why did this come to pass?
To provide them with a derriere
at last!
*

The Buddhists came mumbling
"Sit on your bum."
I did but it wasn't fun
when I sat on my gun.
*

The Muslims came saying
pray 5 times a day
while you face Mecca,
but I couldn't find it
while tossing in the hay.

Fondling Music

Words have been my fondling noise
that never quite turned into music
though song was the ideal I could look at
somewhere in the field of alfalfa or cotton
or by the creek in the mountains.
Illusive song telling me my profession was wrong.
But I could say something almost as if I was talking
    the speech music
        all along
or rather plain ole talkin' funny.

What Turns Here & Now

As what turns
I turn, or bend
as what bends
bends *with*
bent *by*.
The freedom
of electricity
to douse my brain
bending, turning, connecting
to erase thoughts, transmit
in every chapter, every day
of the page, the page of my brain
as stacked, chapters
a book of electric thoughts
3 dimensional where
it can be read from either end
or the middle out
every day stacked
into weeks into months
seasons, years a life
of book thinkings
authorless books
timeless weeks and years
of bending turning thoughts
backwards, forwards forgetting
remembering rejoining
reading, hearing writing
forward or back
end to beginning to beginning
as time threading through all
the container in the library
that extends out bending, turning
in the library the endless
depository, the holding
and moving on of seasons, years
every place the chapters
the paragraphs

the millennia of time
of endings turning
universal dance depository
of dancing through the books
backwards forwards
the content of years
of this second, the word
and phrase
this minute of consciousness
this lifetime of seasons,
beginnings and endings
the attempt to stop is fruitless
the release to move is fruitful
bending, turning, erasing,
remembering
the endless composing
backwards and forwards
from beginning to end and back
from the center out seasons
and chapters, letting the light in
of morning, what was the night
what is the word or words
of the day, carefully crazily
transmitted here and now.

Tired of Living?

Tired of living?
Got your feet stuck on the wall?
Do you hear strange nothings?
Why are you flying through rooms
    sad you have no wings?
Swallowed a pill bigger than your mouth?
Laughed your last laugh?
Lost your last tooth?
Do you snore while awake?
Does life seem full of time?
Are your itches involuntary and unreachable?
Has someone hid everything yet there's nothing to find?
Are you happening in reverse yet getting older?
Does hair seem unnecessary?
Have zeros disappeared?
Does laughter seem sad?
Then you may be suffering from terminal reality.
Watch your every non-step.

Underlying Love

No truer statement is underlying love
as the distant tribes have walked here
over the trails of joy and tears
or to where you are everybody's moving foundation
even on the run – as if anyone could avoid saying love
or its endless equivalents.
Clan moiety group family commitments
as ancient as snow, as warming as seasons
as fruitful as almost any landing place.

It builds in a relationship till it defies description
underlying everything we do, oh partnership
in touching each other renewing in that long trek here.
Or here for so long, what is it that your feelings transport
from room to room or outside in and here to
    furthest outside –
the building of a friendship in trust through setbacks, sickness
the underlying shares rare, necessary, taken for granted never,
when eyes are open, and hands and hearts pulse in memory
and real honest time. 2 connect, 3, 4 maybe only 2
or none, but the parental trek here was full of it
binding necessity – what flood or conflict comes
to drive us on – if it accelerates all that matters
is that facilitator, dependable norm – underlying love
in transit or in place with it, amazing how
distance only supports it, calls to it as we progress
together warding off deceit, greed, tyranny –
generalized forever in its specifics.

The Bounds of Love

To accept a relationship as it is
without wanting more
is impossible –
the bounds of love are not entrapped.
They range and range and range.

Why Tell Him

Tell him what truth is.
    Does he kiss it?
He kisses hell.
Tell him what love is.
    Does he feel it?
He twists it to sex.
Tell him what caring for others is.
    Does he do it?
He sucks all into his empty soul.

The Culture of Sweep

The culture of sweep.
The mystery
come tiny heart.
Unknown known.
Is everything in concordance with flesh?
Who states what is wrong?
Is there a rational beginning to irrationality?

Take it, says power.
Give it up, says hope.
You can't fight the monster
that supercedes David's Goliath
picking at it in little pieces
doesn't even get to its Achilles heel.

The titans of greed are the new Pantheon
our oblique mythology
aslant to Nature.
They'd rather have their god than something else.
Nature fizzles out in their diseased minds.

Hills of Tech

Nothing admires like the hills of tech
programmed to admire itself.
Programed to smile tech smiles through every disaster.

Moon

I often wonder what the perfect light is
everyone has their own color
but are they all the same light
interrelatedness destroys antagonism,
hyper dawn, your moon is my heart.

Blockage?

Why can't I write. Why can't I be there with you.
In spirit since distance destroys.
Why can't I be there in the distance with you.
Why can't I write that, or anything else.
Is anything else in the way with my being
in spirit there with you. As anyone knows
no one knows how to be there in spirit
with you as if the mind could
plant me there, sent in the mail or
on mind waves to be there in an instant
with you on demand or willed or wanted
if ever in need the will is the way
I'm writing you I'm being there with you.

Hurting Out

Why does he hurt so much that he hurts out.
Having led a life of excess why is he so empty?
Why the deprivation of so many so he can have so much?
Does it deprive oneself to be so out of balance
and on top of everything and everything so full
that all that excess drains away and means nothing
and so to lash out to others supposedly lesser
becomes the norm, having so much and feeling so little
it belittles, it denies, it drains, it demotes
until nothing is left but a shell, a broken shell.

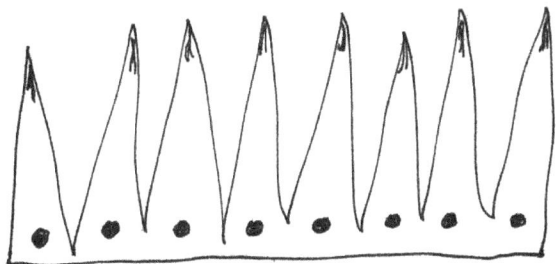

Answers

Are you aware of the sun splitting open the moon?
I haven't looked outside lately.
Or that cyclone that took away Nebraska.
Well now I haven't clicked on my news app for a long time.
What do you think about all those candidates running for office?
Is it November already?
What do you think about arming the entire border with Mexico?
Excuse me I just got a text from UPS.

Recompense

    Power clock, genius of connection, hum of the norm,
    monumental praise of the fittings of the descending universe
    ascending in all directions that go out from each other —

Does anything fit the puzzle except everything that is
as we laughingly and derisively avoid the subject
so we can fight our internecine wars and thrill to pettiness
killing the hands spread out to us and poisoning the bed given us –
we of rich potential, cracked in our thinking and cooperative failures.

Is there any way to forgive our marching egos, our allowing
    authoritarian nightmares
entry to our sacred most selves, our city and state and nation hearts
as we furiously multiply, worshiping our one species to sickness?
We are the lone manipulators of our manufactured poison.

Forgive but how can we forgive after going too far, creating maelstrom
    of marching seas, burning air, heat killing crops and annihilation of
        innocent species.
Where is the recompense after we entered this damaged world of
    our own making, the gates closed behind us?   /29Jun#1

Pulling Through

Pull through, spirit of the pull-throughs.
That last little glimmer left *be* the glimmer left
as suddenly, within that tiny light the spirit of innovation
fires an imagination punctuation of minor proportions
that goes beyond itself into a creative fire
like an evolutionary burst, a turn unpredicted –
fire fire fire firing itself, glow glow glow glowing
into light lighting itself, all spirits combined into
its own little big bang, a little turn for the better, renewed
reviewing itself, going creative-viral, as this radical
reformulation seeming out of nowhere is
each in his own way feeling it, finding it support,
this new healthy warmth, the mystery kicker, the bolt
of alive inspiration suddenly within everyone
the spin out, the spin off, the whirling light energy of
this is what we do!   /29Jun#2

Want: A Human Being Speaks

"I want what I shouldn't want so bad it's beyond want. It follows me even when I leave it behind or if I run from it. I find it before me waiting for me and I run into it thinking I got rid of it.

Want lives screaming and surrounds & pushes through and I deny it knowing I am fooling myself. But want wants itself and wants all over again wanting to want more & more & more with no end in sight since there's no fulfillment for want. It is an attraction to need and sleeps in need's bed, twins of futility. Forever the attractor, the magnet to the vacuum hurt of itself. Want is wanting since it is all want, want is as old as old Norse, Old English, older, taking up residence in some more than others.

It is just there going in and out of desire like a mirror of itself in which nothing is seen because it is want, wanting, wanting badly, so very badly and that nothing that is itself takes over! and becomes the permanent resident of itself of myself as it always has been, simply myself, it and me one person, one vivid want." /8Jul2019

Lufu Lubo Liebe

I love what I should since love defends all and love is all.
All love extends to itself and out endlessly, it seems loving too much
is not enough if the fever takes over into love sickness
but even the extreme of love never encounters hurt or it is not love.
Love perfects itself into God as God fuses into love and becomes love
as love trespasses reason and becomes its own sacred being.
Being *in* love, love surpasses itself, loving only. That could only be
a good thing as the need for a godhead crumbles in its wake,
the boat to the farther shore, the choice often forgotten rediscovered.
If one person drains it it can only be picked up again and again
as overuse only stales the user, always someone will pick it up to be
    renewed
as the source of it, *lufu* and old Frisian *luve*, Old High German *luba*
Gothic *lubo,* Indo-European behind Latin *lubet,* pleasing and there
    it is,
libido meaning desire, the desire to be loved, the desire *to* love,
    the pathway to love
being further love, as love simply goes out to the loved, and
    mature love desires no more
but the unleashed going out to, love *freed to be love* as what it is,
love in all its circles of itself and generating out from endless
    source to
endless recipients, love simply defies all and opens the heart to
    the pleasure of living.

Dumpette

Swelled in perfection
the perfection of destruction
"Hit them with noise
fabricate and call it *fabricay.*
Deceiving is succeeding,
machine gun them with the contents of your Pandora's box."

You've released the energy of the wrong energy
of the wrong time which is our time
of the wrong time anytime,
dumping your dump and calling it *dumpette.*

You are a distorter, a stretching beyond reason,
2 rubber bands tied together and stretched to breaking –
that is your brain, snapped.

Disarray, turn everything into turning it out, on, loud
over-deceptive, totally a ruse, a losing
a loss, a laughing non-laughing matter,
a *destruction* of matter, reason, with it
a tearing, a torn, a torn to shreds,
destruction down to every molecule,
quarks croaked, a crock cracked
a crushed lost hope,
violence parading in your celebration of fear,
violence your crowd of worshipers paid to worship,
your worship, your ship is war. Cross-examining you
is like talking to a blimp. You are all gas,
"gas-say" you say, *touché* I say –
you've exploded, burst into flames!
Hello goodby, ultimate aberration,
stinking burnt spittle scattered smoking on the ground.

Goal

Does anybody entity one two three
feel empathy for four five six and beyond?
Does the cold shoulder work best when it comes to numbers?
That is, shove it out of my mind because it's too big?
Or is it one, simply one, a series of ones, goal posts of ones
one-post goal post, every single one, each
waiting for the score: oh I was the aim, me, centered me
and the score was achieved, the world came to my door
because I'm special, I'm so lonely and so free
just to be admired for who I am. You see
I have nothing to do with anybody since the skin ends entity –
one finger held up, an integer, one solid one or negative one
but still *one thing is me,* your single standard, your flagpole
with drooping flag on it, your goal post, *free* and lonely.

Early Riser

I appreciate the dawn, not everything that has gone wrong
antecedents have a way of freshening the spirits
the benevolent blank, that pause that is light and unexpected
the pre-dawn before the glimmer of dawn, hold your breath
move over disconsolate mood, make room for the unknown
the quirky moment, the half-light, the hesitation before more
the intake before real breathing that is a beginning of begin.
Begin by not doing anything, not attaching meaning not
attaching, shot up but at that moment before starting down
floating in space where everything is right, a stasis, honestly
there are no words for it except, without governing,
the face utterly relaxed, quiet simply characteristic calm,
the bad shit in departure almost in surrender, as if a pause could
take over the world and Nature wholly take over and continue
        breathing.   /17Aug2019

Fool at the Edge

Inching closer to the tipping point, tottering topaz crumbling
    under toe
heel slipping teetering but not tottering, wobbling doddering fool
losing the step, the slide the slippery slope not there yet holding back
in space relinquishing and releasing the slip the slide denied,
lost or losing balance the fool guy feeling the strain of not knowing
anything for sure, for sure nothing, idiot, sooth, truth up in the air
or is it everywhere, a spectacle forsooth, floating or slipping
the fool, woebegone, what does he know, does he vacate thoughts
and give up, accept as you fall, the inevitable, or is it a free fall
or a near miss? the fool deliciously poised or is just a pose
posing for the camera and then what, all hell breaks loose?
But in this instance happy-go-lucky, avant-guard, free,
    who is to know
knowing nothing or is the all passing through and tipping
hit by the all, the force pushes, or caught in the light just one light
    moment   hesitant.

Archival Laughter

Make sure there's plenty retrospection in your laughter
past shades of funnier times, otherwise
you may not laugh at all.

In The Air

Peace where did you go, out the window playing with
    your neighbors?
Who are your neighbors, joy and cooperation?
You're so invisible these days, so transparent even flippant
or, seemingly, a figment of the imagination.
Peace are you a figment? A figtree on a mountain?
A lowly fig? Or just a mountain invisible in the sunset of doom,
the heavy doors closing on you as the last ray diminishes.

Greed, corporate monstrosity have stamped you out
    with a heavy fist.
The human species' thirst for power as more and more suffer
    for the specialized over-pomp few.
Peace has been sucked dry by the unleashed military guns
    and weapons
increased bomb making and insane product gorging of drugs
    cyber mechanics trophy palaces and
        perverse costly delvings of
            the rich and infamous.

But why say it, as you dissolve in the predawn darkness – peace
    what a word.
Look it up online or in your heart.
Maybe you'll find it there pairing up with rational intelligence,
an old buddy "common sense," and that saint – "humility."
Are they there together? Let's you and I not go too far
    from their company.
We know who *we* are, we stubborn visionaries,
down to earth workers working to restore
who knows what will return to a weakening heart
    & thoughtful mind –
a compassionate openness, a willingness in the air.

Orion

Orion teach me to fly again.
I've lost my wings I never had but thought I had.
Prove that I can think I have them again –
prove or teach, what's the difference.
I approve and I learn, or should.
I'm not willing to drop the facade, that's it,
that I'm an accumulation of uncertainty
and have to work hard for every bit of space I occupy.
Bungling, going mad, fighting the upstream technology,
deleting progress, redoing, one little task took hours.
What does this have to do with Orion that is so
    prominent right now lifting up the skies
        with its supposed form?
The naming we put on it, in almost limitless light years
    dispersal, the diversity of your real form.
But you hang in power over me and teach me
    as if you could teach
insignificance, the word that horrifies me when it shoves itself
    into my life, teach me
the value of yourself, insignificance.
The flurry of naming such diverse elements and the imagination
    of centuries
giving you form, body, story, myth – actual placement of the 3
    pyramids
on Earth (from the stars in your belt).
You *must* have strength, but Form *only* from *our* solar system
    that we make of you after all.
You could, that is, part of you, explode in a supernova
but for now these close millions of years you teach me
the vastness of the skies as all your legends war with your reality.
You prove I could have wings, as I watch chickadees getting
    bits of bird seed, and tiny hummingbirds
zigzagging in hilarity or is it competition drinking
    the supposed real nectar. →

Just imagination rises with the dawn to obliterate Orion
    and your vast company of stars
and opens everything that proves possibility, what lives the most
    and closest to my breath, literally flying in and out
        of my lungs as I can
            be with it.

Loved, Loved

"A person might even be described
    as a self-contained multiverse." - Aberjhani

The Sun taking a shower.
Whatever comes to me will be my pedigree.
Now you may doubt my source, as I do.
Two molecules drop together in a DNA.
And suddenly maybe simultaneously on Galaxy XYZ
there comes a call as there's already a signal from within
on just one of the millions of planets
that said "Now you may doubt my source, as I do."
Like a far distant echo, no, a chorus of two.
Whatever comes to me will be my pedigree.
And then, remember, the Sun taking a shower.
That's impossible, everyone says, including me.
Oh Love, let us warm to one another again
friend to friend, relative to relative, lover to lover,
    loved, loved.

The Now of Good

1.
A clear drink has no pouring.
Scotch and divine paradise are misnomers.
Having your legs crossed provokes iniquity.
A good man ruffles hairs,
a bad man is Clorox.
The eternal way is backwards thoughts
so walk forward carrying your indifferences
to what pops in your face.

2.
Read with skepticism.
Speak with Silence.
If you live in the valley
go halfway up the mountain and look back.
If what you see pleases you
let it go.
If what you see disgusts you
you might be in the right place.

3.
Peace of mind is as flat as a pancake.
Love is round as an Apple.
How round is round and how long is an apple?
How flat is flat and how peaceful is a pancake.
Eliminating all is a good breakfast.
Therefore not seeing anything is a first for enlightenment.

4.
He who manufactures lust by
staring at it all day
deserves its vacuum.
Emptiness takes over both sides of full.
So remember what cups you
what saucers you
and be grateful for what's on your plate.

If you work hard enough you'll have
something to eat.
If you do nothing
you'll have plenty to share.

5.
The way is bigger than my path,
wider than any road.
The way winds beyond the trail you are on
and laughs at thoroughfares and highways.
If you don't move you are on the way.
If you move you are equally fulfilling.
The way does not grasp you nor can you grasp it.
Nature shows you the way whether
    you look or not.

6.
Knowing what's in front of you
doesn't free the mind.
Knowing what's in back of you does.
Knowing what's on the right side of you
doesn't free the mind.
Knowing what's on the left of you does.
Knowing what's above you
doesn't free the mind.
Knowing what's below you does.

Knowing what's at the center of you
doesn't free the mind.
Knowing what's not at the center of you
does
Knowing all the colors of the rainbow
doesn't free the mind
knowing the darkness underlying it
does.

Fall/Winter Trends

The Hunter Greens can't stand the Purples
    let alone the Pistachios as the battle ensues.
The Shocking Pinks are no longer out in front
    but the Cherry Reds are hot and striving forward.
Whisky Browns are after them unisex, mono-sex, multi-sex
    any way they can.
Digital Blues hate it as the Fuchsia Pinks arm themselves
    to the teeth compensating violently
    while the Lavenders watch on in passive disgust.
Here come the Oranges who can't stand any of the others –
they hate the Sapphire Yellows and abhor the Olive Greens
    that were so much in vogue last year.
Marble Gray and Silver are not to be left out forging ahead
    of the Hunter Greens and Purples and trouncing the Lavenders.
What are we going to do with the Fall and Winter colors?
Fashion of the Rich is at War.

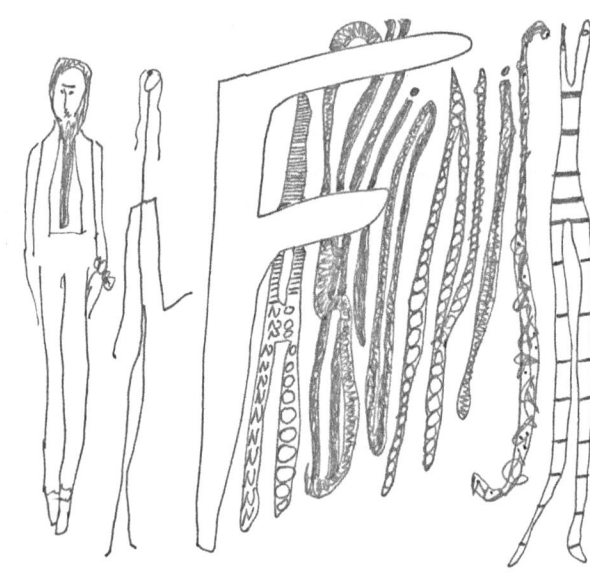

Worse Than Any Skunk

It broke and what was left but the broke?
Broken energies, feverish discussions
disavowals, tripping over one's feet in public,
the private parading as public, the confusion all set in.
The cake baked like a hard sell, no thank you,
I don't want your rotten product, your lack of anything
approaching truth. Those who follow you
are leading with their ass.
All connections are lost except with corruption.
Corruption and lying, the egg that popped open, a dead chick.
From birth on, every door toward blame and fame.
Cheat, steal, fuck. Mobster mayhem. Self-contaminated
by self again. It broke, it broke, what was left
but the broken. A rotten egg smell worse than any skunk.
A smell to bring down the world if we let it.

A Peach

In snitty feech
a peach of a peach
a peach I trust –
impeach. Delicious to eat impeach
and not throw up impeach.
In snitty feech and seek
and seek and seek impeach
impeach has nothing to do with peach
impeach.   /10oct2019

Joseph E. Tweezers

See through to great poetry.
See what the dog says.
We have no dog.
See through, saw through,
what is the dust
that's on my eyeballs
that's covered your mind
and your hind legs.
I'm not a rabbit.
I wash off with a washrag
every morning.

I'm Joseph E. Tweezers
looking for poetry.
Yes without me there is no me
and you wouldn't exist, Mr. Tweezers.
You'll never find it there
where you're looking.
You're looking for something
most people don't care about.
I thought I saw something
on the other side of the page
that's backwards and crossways.
That's why I'm interested –
I can't make it out
but it has variable lines.
I turned the page over
and one of the lines was
"stories within stories stories"
That's why people don't give a child's cry
for poetry. It's too vague and has no meaning.
You and your dog and your rabbit.

Cacophony of Music

Oh the world the world of worlds
what is within the world
rolling ever rolling rolling
tossed and held through space
mythologies clustered on you
from the people abound
stories within stories stories
bound to and from their speakers
their listeners the believers and non-believers
keeping them alive.
From the stress of Cain to the compassion of
Pautiwa to the stories bred from *science*
– the most compelling of all –
the wonders of the world hearing everything at once.

Death of a Hummingbird

Where is that ecstatic verbatim
where one has time to listen
where you listen to your forebearers
bears on fours
and the hummingbird's spirit
the tapping of rain on the roof.

Game

My head is full of dice.
Someone keeps picking them up, two by two,
and throwing them against my skull.
Is it the 2 hands of my soul?
The left and the right?
The eternal duality
that we're supposed to transcend?
It is impossible to throw a one.

Who It Is

Love undefined a silhouette unknown
what pulls at consciousness
never lets go once grabbed
pulls down down down is in every room,
outside among the fruit trees, on the portal
next to the spruce, as tall as the spruce,
as small as what's sitting beside me in the porch swing.
What is most touching can't be touched.
Comes in from a friend's voice or the imagined memory,
no memory is really real so
what is it daily compelling, this love ghost
this real presence that is not real except feeling.
What do you feel, do you feel it.
Is it someone you knew or someone you know,
what exactly is the who it is?
Why does it lie across my life like
an endless longing?   /18Oct2019

It is Me, I Write It Down in the Air!
- Paul Blackburn

Play on, sky of tomorrow,
your adventures on to eternity
as I part with my part
and somehow my mind carries on
to full disclosure.

12 Step Breath

Is Dharma colored
and Karma an old man?
Dharma is black
and Karma white.

Is the oldest of old
older than the oldest old
and the new is that.

Is a mean man mean
and a woman kind
and going to win out.

Or are all stakes pulled out
and a ghastly spirit free
to roam and win.

Is there no battle
and after all the deaths and misery,
peace erased it all?

Wars piled on wars
and faced reality –
two shoes on one foot
is no good.

Is sex confused with sperm
and the egg too popular.
Is Mr. Hormone queer?

Is the planet a giant merchandise
in God's garage sale?
And covered with aphids?

Does Earth reject all this
including its human inhabitants.
Let them swim with the fish
that are left.

Who's going to take out the trash?
Hispanics are golden, so are Blacks,
Whites not so golden
after the Native American gold.

Is the richest the poorest
as meanwhile we exist
in a 12-step middle ground
poor, just like eternity.

Is a higher donkey
a power you can't hee haw
so relaxation remains ever
a first.

After Thoughts

The flowers that face the world are dead
and I'm dead under them.

―――――

He threw his spirit at the wind
and it blew back at him.

―――――

He faced the exact time of his death
which was 4 o'clock on Saturday
just in time for church on Sunday.

Greed Über Alles

Greed redistributed among too many
taken to a high pitch and farmed out to the wealthy,
the wealthiest overpopulation
in explosion, the gooey gummy shit of it infesting everything.
Only money
won't buy your way out of hell now.

What Happened

       You know, it's all gonna stop
         when the top stops spinning
           as the audience is encapsulated in a gentle hand
         and the playboys stop dreaming of lost nights
       dawns break through the white boys' mechanisms
     and money in a great big dollar sign
   falls flat and crumbles.
The rotation comes to a standstill and much
to the horror of every living being
      nothing moves and with a strange creaking noise
  it all slowly starts out the opposite direction –
    flags, buildings, jungles, zoos
        chickadees and farmers and native grasses
      backwards turning faster gathering speed
    guess what, we're all spinning again
   but in the opposite direction.

Welcoming Signs

I keep looking for the news I want to read to no avail.
Most of it comes right up to the edge   and falters
as I turn back disappointed.
How can you follow a non-leader?
How can you make the news
    be news you want more than anything to hear?
I could strive to *make* news
but that wouldn't be good for anyone or good for me.
So I wait with my preformed ideas of compelling news.
News that some things seriously major
    have been put back in place . . . so they work again.
News of a lessening of abusive intent and dominating dumbness
that the cracks in hubris and poisonous ego have penetrated
    and the ghastly asshole-ism is breaking apart
the hulk of hypocrisy and self-indulgence
    is disintegrating!
And the world Earth is speaking to everybody
and through less crashing religions people
get down on their knees to heal the Earth
and stop getting in the way   of the Earth healing itself.
There is no news today that I want to hear or read or see
except in isolated spirits of protest, welcoming signs.

Fake Manikin

Success turns humans into display manikins
fat unembraceable ones
detached from Earth-Reality –
bloated weight objects
opposite their seesaw of gold –
"Give me a hundred and ninety pounds
    of diamonds
make it two-twenty, two hundred twenty million.
My millions fold into billions.
What do I care
having thrown up blinders
to poverty?
I speak for all Men Daddies
storming absurdities.
Whatever attire the best of best, give me
I wear as no one else wears,
fit to spit on a king,
despots linking elbows –
dictators kiss both cheeks.
Suddenly I've arrived to paid laughter.
Licking lackeys, slick subservients
wish, all wish, to be *me*" –

a broken-earth face
a poisoned-atmosphere rear
a lead-laced watery eye
oil-slick nose
parched-earth mouth,
a brain where logic failed,
a destiny in the eye of a hurricane,
a penis the size of a dead worm –
white skin made out of oiled plastic
where the heart should be, a metal stub –
a dynamited soul.
    Where compassion should be
a rock-hard ego displaying
display on display on

the corrupt play of pompous
pomp and circuitous.
"Look at what's on me.
Wouldn't you like to have
my gross gross grossness?
my emptiness, my terrifying
hole in the center?"   /28Nov2019

The Winning Soul

Suddenly the soul splits open
and *half* of it descends into the playworld
    of abusive-actions TV and grungy world folly
    into the SM cult of entertainment –
and *the other half* tries to maintain itself
by breathing into simple postures
with the mind wondering what it was doing
but slowing down.

So the *whole* human being was in two parts
that didn't war with itself internally
but simply accepted its two extremes
that had been blown into two, coming apart
just being natural, unnatural in Nature but then
what does Nature know, being the loser.

Slobber Love

I can slobber over you all I want.
It doesn't affect you. You don't know.
My love is as pure and intense as daylight.
It makes no demands.
It gives me comfort, a fantasy based on reality that isn't fantasy
    but an enlarged reality,
a selfless steady outgoing that appreciates, no end,
what you give to it, the *trust you* give back,
little knowing what voice you give to your everyday living
is like manna to my soul, adds the companionship to my life
that holds *isolation* at bay, erases it with new presence,
a partnership on Earth among its inhabitants –
which is rare and shouldn't be, among all the isolated souls,
it becomes permanent in its fragility, its one way out to paradise –
my way, my one way love, just as potent as anything
holding the day up in sunlight.

The Center

    The center from which all comes
    long sense faded into distance
    that is so far it is irretrievable.

    Wait for the facts?

    I imagine so.

    Or has it now dispersed
    into untold billion centers
    totally retrievable
    to all who pause
    and allow their own
    evidence of it
    to appear.

Shouting At The Muse

Nothing seems to come to me anymore, stark like a lightning bolt.
I want sudden energies, grabbed collars and face in my face.
"Here's what you're going to say and say it now!"
Instead the day waxes into waning and time dribbles out.
Repetition throws me against the wall and says nothing.
Listen here, Spirits, or what were spirits, or an indication of
    something greater than myself,
where are you? How have I abandoned you when I need you?
What in me repulses? Is it time to know myself? Do I have time to
    start all over again?

How To

How to get rid of belly fat.
Get a plastic vat
and put belly fat in that
and work at that.

How to cross your eyes.
Take one eye in left hand
the other in right,
cross them over
but don't tie optic nerves
in knots.
Look at that.

How to sing freely.
Open mouth and utter.
Utter at different pitches.
Utter and utter,
utter loud and low.
Don't stop uttering.

How to beat a cow.
Take a beet with leaves on it.
Hold beet stems and swing at cow.
Follow cow if cow moves.
Keep beating.
You have beat a cow.

How to tie your shoe.
This takes fantasy.
Take one shoe and another shoe
in another hand.
Go through tying motions with both
shoes in hand.
You have shoes in a tie.

      OR

Run with shoes in hands.
Stop running with shoes held out
equally before you.
Your shoes are tied.

How to drop a coin.
Pinch coin between thumb and first finger.
Hold straight out from body.
Release pinch.
Coin will drop.
If coin doesn't drop
you have a wonder.

How to find your crotch.
Take right hand
or left if left handed.
Let it drop down hanging freely.
Swing over to left
or right if left handed.
Don't swing too far.
Press back against your body.
You have found your crotch.
It's not someone else's.

How to misfire a gun.
Hold your gun tightly.
Make sure it is loaded.
If you don't have a gun
go on to next set of directions.
Bang gun on back of chair
or any solid object
until it misfires.
If it doesn't misfire
you haven't banged enough.

Next set of directions.
This set is self-contained.
It sets its own directions.
Simply do nothing with
the next set of directions.

How to piss off a Mormon.
Tell a male Mormon
he must marry another male Mormon
or he will go to Hell.
Or tell a female Morman
she must marry another female Morman
or she will go to hell.

How to stop writing nonsense.
If you write it and it doesn't make sense
chances are it is nonsense.
If you stop writing what makes no sense
then you've stopped writing nonsense.

Stop writing nonsense.

Honor

When is the unstomachable unstomachable
and you become turnyourbackonable?
Even if it's not honorable to be turnyourbackonable
at least too much turnyourbackonableness
could isolate you into egomaniacal
turnyourbackonable dishonorableness.
So face the disgusting with all your heart and soul
and become totally throwupable again.

Dreaming

I was dreaming there was a sky
underneath my pillow
and I'd woken up from
the dream I'd just had.
I will try
to be open to reality
more
lovely every day.
✛
As the great authors
marched toward extinction
the musicians accompanied them
and the artists
the scientists
and just about everybody else
and lastly, most guilty of all,
the politicians
dragging their feet.
✛
Life is an adventure
of floating downward
to the crust of the Earth
and living there
impolitely.

Unheeded Advice

Go ahead
be peripheral
strike onions with fish
pump meaning into words
in your arguments.
Dare to dance
on top of the world
upside down in a
reversed frenzy.
Peaches into ploughshares
throwing off tomatoes
be an old shoe
and throw that too.
Are you happy
as you stop dancing
sit up or is it
sit down?
Why not surround yourself
with a half-eaten
rainbow?
Kiss your daughter.
Provide something
central.
Shine through.

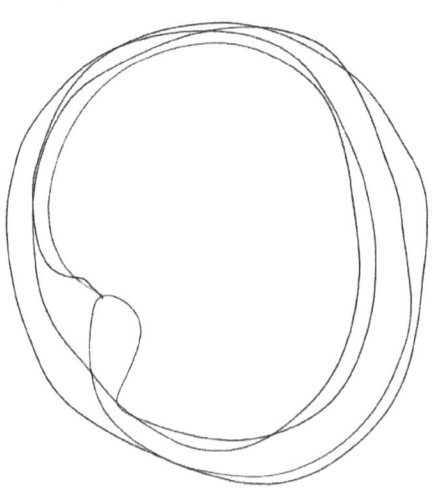

It Is Free

    It is curious, isn't it
    the light we carry with us
    which follows in the dark
    even when let go.
    Something which shines
    even when covered up
    or it sings its own song
    "grace."

I don't want to hear it
or see it
in such moments
when I wallow in my own
familiarity.

    But if I move a bit
    into a new space
    where letting go
    is present
    something penetrates . . .
    I don't have to carry
    or think about
    or see.

Where is it when it is
where it is.
It is flesh of my flesh
in spirit.
Everything I thought about it
was untrue.
It's no different
from me.

Have We Been Here?
We Have Been Here
/for Wayne Jones, 80 years

Have we been here
we have been here
you and me and
many others
some came and left.
      Some came with spangles on
left with mud on their boots.
Many came and left.
Remember the Vietnam War
remember the Vietnam Vets
as you are
    who came here
    lived here
left
remember marching down Central
young people, *we* were younger
some pregnant women
    marching
the business people looking at us
    as we walked
and when we danced danced
    in the bar
    to loud and louder bands
some quieter or just a country fiddler
or Ginsberg in a crowd
dancing, chanting, people doing
    uncommon things
the matching and uncoupling of people
the handmade day to day activities
embroidering blue work shirts
long dresses, belly dancing, marriages
love, remember love?
drumming, ignorant chanting
lighting stars on the forehead
out of mind ritual guided drugs

shouting in canyons, marriages
    by the creek or next to red rock canyons
        rock groups from Taos Santa Fe
Albuquerque, throngs for New Years
arts fairs, locally designed booths
    a casita almost a hermitage
renting houses or squatting
turning a place into a magnet for others
much to surprise and confusion and some
    elder dislike of residents –
so many could build unique dwellings –
    didn't yours have a sloping floor?
a commune, hell, just living together
not me but I observed –
doing farming, what's new from California,
    New York, beads leather
    diets changing
    sweats, food stamps
        Tarot, *I Ching*, peyote
poetry readings, photography, art even
    on basement walls, volleyball, most of all
    the music, live music groups
fire station concerts   4th of July
    local real dancers
dancing, we got hitched up
had our own spring-fed swimming pool –
we did all kinds of things, handmade stuff
    up from the ground –
and everything turned over into the commerce
    of growth and we weathered, stayed
or some of us,
many were here anyway,
we were all new and yet long time here
as time robs of youth, the spirit stays
stays on year after year

festival after festival, dance after dance
plan after plan, job to job, place
      to place within a place, this place
   of little places, we come and we go
in a village, and some died many died
and we're living now families of families
changing growing up generations generating
and children from tiny to teen to adult
as different unwanted unneeded wars
come and go and we're stuck here
with the gangster wealthy gone mad
as we weather another political storm
with still our integral spirit
singing the song of the Earth the Fathering Sun
the urgency of the local informed by
      the local
it presses on to celebration do you hear
that music which is this music
the heart beat of memory in this circle of
   love and cooperation to get things done
the theater we had is the theater
      we are.
Have we been here we have been here
   you and me and many others
some came and left
many came and left, many stayed
   and here we are
we have been here and
   here we are.

"If music be the food of love, play on;
 give me excess of it . . ."
      - William Shakespeare in"Twelfth Night)

Republican Counsel & Congressman

(watching impeachment proceedings)

"Who ordered the larger than normal shoe size for your Grandmother Tillie? Was it your sister Floozy Sue or Colonel Roundrump? Who ordered that shoe size, don't beat around the bush, was it your nephew Pete Pot? Or your half-brother Flatto Braino? Who? And how many times did you order larger than normal shoe sizes for Grandmother Tillie? More than once? A dunce of times, two hundred and 80? Who did it? Remember you're under oath. Or was it Crosseyed Creepo your flatfooted neighbor's son? Or was it you, you pint-sized platypus? Was it you?" – Republican Lawyer

"I would like to follow up on the report that legerdemain was used during the President's trips to the bathroom. Do you deny your trickery in removing the floor under the President's feet, even though temporarily, so that he stumbled on the way to the John? Also there's evidence you practiced avoirdupois surreptitiously to deflect him from his normal toiletry procedures. If you deny this how do you explain the absence of Herr Presidente's morning tweet?" – Republican Lawyer

"Who is most important in these proceedings? The Fartblower. The single most important basis for all the stench that's going on, the confusion and the muck. Without the identity of the Fartblower we know nothing. We demand the Fartblower as witness. If we don't know Mr. Fartblower we know nothing. WHO IS THE FARTBLOWER?" – Republican Lawyer

"An election is an election of Great Pith and Pissident Putin is our avowed leader affirmed by our God of the Mystic Pantaloons and Prevalent Penis Party. Any attempt at removal of our Heilistic Master of No Reproach is an abominable act of Tritchery. God bless our White Mixmaster Pissident Putin and may he trounce all dissidents who steal the roses from his Sacred Path." – Republican Congressman

He Did It

"He did it but it wasn't a big did, it was a little did."

But he did do it and that is all that matters.

"He did what he does all the time so what's the big deal, it's a little did that's often done."

But the very fact that he did do it is enough. It is a major did.

"No, a minor one, an often done did, a trivial did."

It is a big whopping thing to do, an illegal even traitorous thing, an unpatriotic fucked up evil petty self-privileging horrible thing to do that is the worst possible example of presidential behavior imaginable and a terrible affront on democracy, the rule of law, a poisonous deed embarrassing to our country and all other democratic leaders and their countries.

"A little teeny did done by someone who can do nothing wrong."

A Note From Busy Barb

"Jimmy Jordin juiced on puppy dog pit bull attack bile spitting smelly pellets of distortions, obstructions and lies, keep it up oh Young Republican Dingleberry. Oh Praise Petro-Billionaires, NR Asses, Koch Sucker Freaks, and all the Morbidly Wealthy of America, you are our taxlessly Rich Gods. Oh Praise White Hat Cultist and Primo Occultist, Mighty Toilet Tweeter of America, may your Fat Sacred Hypocrisy and Smarmy Lies prop up your Billowing Fat forever." – Busy Barb, Your Sex-for Favor Republican Consort

Candle 1

A prayer for the prayerfully neglected
in the darkness with the light
that's denied hardly to be reached
the glimmer beginning, a turn around
the light glancing off the key of willingness.
                /Winter Solstice & 1st Day of Hannakuh

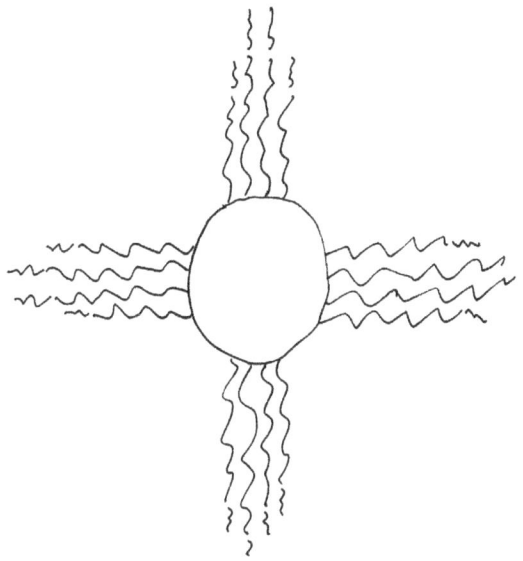

Candle 2

Blessed are you, the Spirit of the Universe, before and after, now and never, during and furious and timeless, forming out of yourselves one, and out of one many. Eons of going on preciously giving us a Now to live in and Love from Stars to Solar to Earth, from Earth to Residents, light centered, focused real, burning through the goodness of Ancestors, the one source of each other refreshing in our minute scale –
families, ancestors, progressions into all species, all life, all neighbors - plants and animals - lit in peace at their best as the best is now in activism for good and sustainable planet Earth. This light turns night into day, the gift of new day breaking even in evening night.

Desert Song

Rain sounding the seeds of tomorrow
gentle on the roof, this late December
when we need it most.
That beautiful snow topping the Sandias
can get refreshed.
As the world fights within itself
and religions try to best each other,
we stay with the normalcy of the local
even that in jeopardy.
Cool forces of Winter, stay with us
and let the sound of dancing particles
rain on the roof, snow on the mountain
be our song.

End
COMMONS

COMMONS
Poems 2017 - 2019

A Patchwork of Enigma 128
A Time To Open My Heart 39
A Normal Day 51
A Place of Skulls 79
A New Leaf 178
A Peach 207
A Note From Busy Barb 230
Absent 153
Accident Pleasure 106
After Thoughts 213
Ah 114
America's Problem 147
Among All Colors 36
An Offer 68
Anal Party 155
Answers 193
Arch Directive 23
Archival Laughter 200
Artichokes of Pluperfect Gods 10
As The Stars Tell 167
Baron Fracas Von Fuckus 17
Bathroom Humor 49
Be The Light Within 108
Be Be 15
Beast 180
Belief 96
Belled Out 166
Best Shared 69
Birth Of Song 26
Blockage? 192
Brat's Notes 155
Brotherly 44
Brothers and Sisters 119
Bye Bye Dogma 166
Bye Bye Net neutrality 94
Cacophony of Music 209
Candle 1 231
Candle 2 231
Cheap Shots 48

"Citizens United" 21
Church of Reality 61
Closest One 90
Collusion 80
Common As the Rare 74
Conversations 115
Criminal Crapola 117
Critique 25
Curiosity 149
Dark Interior 112
Dark Father 36
Dawn Song 97
Dawn or Not 29
Death of a Hummingbird 209
Death Thinking 37
Deception 118
Deflation 130
DeKooning Buddhism 136
Democracy 132
Desert Song 232
Did You Say Garden? 134
Directions 167
Diversity 122
Do Not Give Up Football 176
Don't Do It 24
Door To Door 78
Dreaming 223
Dumb Fuck 153
Dumpette 198
Early Riser 199
Earth in Oligarchal Grip 18
Educate 23
End Times 80
Etiquette 2018 147
Ever Present 163
Exactly the Same 162
Exiles 65
Fairy Tale: Beast of Zozar 46
Fake Manikin 216

Fall/Winter Trends 206
Family Tale 229
Felicitous Dharma 55
First One 157
Fizznew 93
Flavor of Innocense 113
Fondling Music 187
For Kathy. 28
For Lenore 121
For Ann 73
Fragile Grace 68
From Memory 151
Game 210
Gentle Rain 148
Get It Right With Him 142
Getting Low 85
Gift of Unknowing 50
Go On 39
Goal 199
Going Forward 130
Going In, Getting Out 43
Good Hands 128
Good Morning, Prayer – 92
Gravitational Waves 106
Greed Über Alles 214
Guiding Eyes 156
Gun Down 129
Half Wish 83
Hallelujah 116
Handshake 107
Harvest 38
Have We Been Here? 226
He Did It, 232
He 126
He Did It 230
Healing Time 145
Here We Are 144
Here and Now 103
Heterosapien 133
Hills of Tech 192
HONOR, The Winning Soul 214
Honor 222
Hormonal Blast 110

How To 220
Hubba Hubba 21
Hurting Out 193
I Couldn't Lie 186
Immensity 121
Impetus On 47
Impossibly Blue 176
In The Air 201
In Love 116
In The Valley 141
In Good Hands 158
Inflated Doodad 168
It is Me I Write It Down 211
It Is Free 225
It's Better to Love 109
Joseph E. Tweezers 208
Jot 6
Journal Page 124
Judge Brat Year of the Man 154
June 6th & On 34
Keep the Poor from the Door 20
Known To Be Known 137
Lack Of 13
Leaving Roswell 152
Less Rotten New Year 172
Lie the Truth to Death 22
Like Me 85
Listening to Schoenberg 122
Loner Freedom 126
Longing 34
Looking For Common Sense 1
Loss Is Gain 177
Love in Quotes 127
Love Unfolds 162
Loved, Loved 203
Loving Someone 100
Lufu Lubo Liebe 197
Machismo 71
Mantra Of Care 91
Masculine Spirit 95
Matriarchs: A Note 72
Meditations Under Venus 40
Meeting Jim Fish 35

Miss Malfunction 16
Mitosis 66
Mono Color 102
Moon 192
Moral Ground 2
Moralitee 184
Morning Star - 17 Poems 34
Morning 98
Mother of Vast Decree 174
Mother of Ancient God 19
Mother Nature 125
Mountain Top 77
Ms. Nature 114
Musing About It 118
My Derriere 187
Mystery Caller 182
Myth Mother 64
Nature Itself 146
Nature's Miracle Pill 131
No Muse 43
No Nada 150
Noise Bank 82
Not Too Late 67
Not Camping 37
October 24 75
Oh Aurora 140
On The Physical 109
On Laboring at Meditation 156
One to Another 108
One More Year 135
Ongoing 70
Open to Secret 170
Orion 202
Particles of Wisdom 112
Phoenix - From the Ashes 45
Poet Power 14
Poetica Pills 131
Pop Music 112
Pray(se) 138
Primary 118
Pulling Through 195
Qué Pasa Picasso? 58
Queen Of Everything 171

Rainbow Speaking 161
Recompense 194
Reflection of the Universe 181
Repair 60
Repetition 77
Republican Counsel 229
Rescue Next To You 157
Return Home 62
Scattering Voice 104
Scimitar 47
Secretly I Love Openly 136
Shouting At The Muse 219
Silence 134
Slobber Love 218
Solo Dancer 156
Song Chant: Truth to Tell 230
Spica They Tell Me 179
Stealth Bombers 22
Step Breath 212
Students 119
Suddenly the Sky Falling 60
Superb Be 7
Swell Fire of Light 5
Talk It Out 120
Teeter-Totter 200
Tense 76
That Humility 180
The Song In You 96
The Bruisers 71
The Culture of Sweep 191
The Dawning – 2018 123
The Light Bounces Through 97
The Bounds of Love 190
The Now of Good 204
The Fountain Of No Muse 56
The Bruisers 108
The Winning Soul 217
The Older You Get 9
The Harmony of Tao 52
The Center 218
The Mind Carries On Love 137
The Ghastly Remains 20
The Last Violator 2

The Learning Curve of Death 111
They Threw Me Out 103
They All Have Mothers 166
They're Glad You're Poor 79
This Room 84
This Will Only Take A Minute 3
Through The Trees 30
Tired of Living? 189
To Speak About Love 4
Too Late 35
Transmission 81
Tufts 177
Tums 83
Uh Oh 183
Unconscious Sonnet 28
Underlying Love 190
Unheeded Advice 224
Unstuck 143
US Is the Underbelly 143
Venus Warns 41
Vowels and Vows 54
Waking Up Too Early 54
Walking On My Bones 176
Want: A Human Being 196

Water Chant 101
Water Creek Swallowtails 99
We Know Nothing 181
We Sonnet 76
Wealth Sickness 161
Wealthy Healthy Says 23
Welcoming Signs 215
What Who 42
What Am I Going to Do 12
What To Do 183
What Is Love 127
What Was Our Face 111
What Happened 214
What Turns Here & Now 188
What Is the Screw 132
What Tragedy? 65
Who I Am Not 17
Who It Is 211
Why Tell Him 191
Wishful Thinking 165
Worse Than Any Skunk 207
Wrong Direction 50
You And I 86
Youthful Gain, 152

Free Speech Poetry

Free Speech Poetry is in almost every locality. It's at odds or even oblivious to traditional national or international poetry. A good part of it flourished in and out of slam renewing the Ginsberg/New American Poetry Revolution which continues on. Free Speech Poetry is vital in its reading performance lead more in larger cities, but all over I'm sure. Publish on demand services such as KDP bring books out from cooperative friends and individuals doing the typing editing layout. Locality ignites poets because of availability of live poetry events. Open readings and/or featured readers are the venue. Proliferation of poetry books by poets themselves assures locality even when poets go places exploring venues of other non-establishment poets. The locality of publication is the result of being ignored by both the East and West Coast publisher and university establishments. And there's the dive in book reading and closing of book stores. When you get down to it, all poetry is local. A good time to co-op to the co-ops.

My commentary on "extensions of poetry" and some early work are here thanks to "Dispatches from the Poetry Wars." https://www.dispatchespoetrywars.com/author/larrygood/

Some Fellow Do-It-Yourselfers

(in good company editing publishing our own work)

William Blake, Robert Bly, Lord (George) Byron, Stephen Crane, e.e. cummings, T.S. Eliot, Robinson Jeffers, Rod McKuen, William Morris, Edgar Allen Poe, Alexander Pope, Ezra Pound, Carl Sandburg, Percy Bysshe Shelley, Gertrude Stein, Alfred Lord Tennyson, Walt Whitman and thousands more recently.

Recent books by the Poet
Nothing To Laugh About - poems 2015-2016
Hot Art & Other Plays 2019
A New Land & Other Writings 2019
@larrygoodell

"The Larry Goodell / Duende Archive is a unique record of the thriving poetry and small press cultures of the Southwest (and New Mexico in particular) from the early 1960s to the present."
http://www.granarybooks.com/collections/goodell/
Steve Clay / Granary Books
now at Beinecke.

Love

"A love still together held key." - from "Unlocked" for Lenore. Lenore Goodell adds a vision of strength to my life, a mature art sense, brilliant art work, and an active appreciation of flowering native flora, presenting the beauty of our planet Earth when left unviolated.

duende press

po box 571 placitas, new mexico 87043
larrynewmex@gmail.com   larrygoodell.com
https://duende.bandcamp.com/

I thank
the Commons.

www.ingramcontent.com/pod-product-compliance
Lightning Source LLC
Chambersburg PA
CBHW020849090426
42736CB00008B/308